Trust Your Mind

Embracing Nuance in a World of Self-Silencing

JENARA NERENBERG

HARPERONE
An Imprint of HarperCollins*Publishers*

This book is designed to give information on various conditions and approaches for your personal knowledge. It is not intended to be complete or exhaustive, nor is it a substitute for the advice of your physician or mental health-care provider. You should seek medical care promptly for any specific medical or mental health condition or challenge you may have.

All efforts have been made to ensure the accuracy of the information contained in this book as of the date published. The author and the publisher expressly disclaim responsibility for any adverse effects arising from the use or application of the information contained herein.

Some names in this book have been changed to protect people's privacy.

HarperCollins books may be purchased for educational, business, or sales promotional use. For information, please email the Special Markets Department at SPsales@harpercollins.com.

FIRST HARPERONE PAPERBACK PUBLISHED IN 2026

Library of Congress Cataloging-in-Publication Data is available upon request.

ISBN 978-0-06-331710-9

Printed in the United Kingdom

26 27 28 29 CPI 10 9 8 7 6 5 4 3 2

Praise for *Trust Your Mind*

"How have we fallen so deeply into groupthink, even in institutions that are meant to facilitate an exchange of diverse views like college campuses? In this highly accessible book, Jenara Nerenberg explains how we got into cul de sacs of dogmatism, and how we can get out of them."

—Eboo Patel, founder and president of Interfaith America and author of *We Need to Build: Field Notes for Diverse Democracy*

"Nerenberg offers ways to speak up, stand alone, and be true to ourselves. . . . Nerenberg's timely and thought-provoking analysis is sure to spark discussion."

—*Booklist*

"A deeply human book that masterfully addresses one of the great problems of our times. Compelling, lucid, and timely, it should be required reading, as it not only explains the complex stew of social psychological forces that have gotten us to this point, but also provides readers with a science-informed blueprint for skillfully navigating the cultural headwinds they face."

—Ethan Kross, international bestselling author of *Chatter* and *Shift*

"*Trust Your Mind* creatively weaves together diverse developments over recent decades to illuminate the causes and impacts of the reduced free speech and increased groupthink that now plague public intellectual life. Her book should inspire renewed appreciation of and engagement in the critical thinking and open discourse that are so essential for the flourishing of individuals and society alike."

—Nadine Strossen, former president of the ACLU and author of *Free Speech*

"*Trust Your Mind* is a bold call to think deeper and speak truer. Jenara Nerenberg shows how self-censorship holds us back from authentic connection and how to combat our habit of self-enforced silence for better conversations, a stronger society, and more personal resilience."

—Kurt Gray, PhD, author of *Outraged* and director of the Deepest Beliefs Lab and the Center for the Science of Moral Understanding

"A perceptive exploration of the forces driving self-silencing, loneliness, and social isolation in a polarized world. Jenara Nerenberg provides a thoughtful guide to reclaiming individuality, embracing nuance, and building authentic connections. A must-read for anyone seeking to navigate modern discourse with clarity and humanity."

—Joel Salinas, MD, co-author of *Conflict Resilience: Negotiating Disagreement Without Giving Up or Giving In*

"As an educator, philosopher, and advocate for liberal learning, I deeply appreciate Nerenberg's rich exploration of the harms of self-censorship and groupthink. She makes a compelling case for thinking for ourselves by seeking out honest, open, courageous, and humble conversations with each other. This book is a welcome intervention in a polarized age."

—Jennifer Frey, professor of philosophy in the Department of Philosophy & Religion at The University of Tulsa

"*Trust Your Mind* is a timely exploration of the downsides of self-censorship and groupthink in a polarized world. Using sharp analysis and research, Jenara Nerenberg guides us all toward opening our minds, engaging in real communication, embracing nuance, and viewing people as the complex, multifaceted individuals that they are—not the identities or ideas we think they're supposed to represent."

—Andrew Boryga, author of *Victim*

Praise for *Divergent Mind*

"Every woman who struggles to flourish in our one-size-fits-all society should read this book."

—Susan Cain, *New York Times* bestselling author of *Quiet*

"*Divergent Mind* explores powerful and positive ways to understand our fundamental differences. Its focus on women is much needed and timely. The book de-pathologizes those of us who most profoundly and intensely think and feel the world around us. I found it to be eye-opening and healing."

—Mary Pipher, *New York Times* bestselling author of *Women Rowing North* and *Reviving Ophelia*

"American psychiatry has increasingly taught our society to think that people can be divided into two categories: those who are 'normal' and those who are 'not normal.' In *Divergent Mind,* Jenara Nerenberg powerfully writes of an urgent need to scrap that way of thinking, and replace it with a societal appreciation for the many gifts that people with divergent minds bring to our world. Hers is a clarion call for change."

—Robert Whitaker, *New York Times* bestselling author of *Anatomy of an Epidemic* and *Mad in America*

"This book is powerful, much-needed for our times, and Jenara Nerenberg offers a unique blend of personal, scientific, and societal analysis. *Divergent Mind* is really for all women, giving them the chance to understand each others' invisible differences and gifts."

—Elaine Aron, PhD, bestselling author of *The Highly Sensitive Person*

"What is 'normal'? Who gets to decide? Jenara Nerenberg's wide-ranging *Divergent Mind* asks and answers these and other essential questions, offering a vision for how individuals and society can take better advantage of the many ways in which we are human."

—Louise Aronson, MD, *New York Times* bestselling author of *Elderhood: Redefining Aging, Transforming Medicine, Reimagining Life*

"This wonderfully positive and accessible introduction to the neurodiversity paradigm is packed with life-changing insight for anyone whose way of experiencing the world diverges from the ordinary."

—Nick Walker, PhD, autistic neurodiversity scholar and aikido teacher

"In this enormously important book, Jenara Nerenberg brings to light the history and lived experiences of a 'lost generation.' . . . *Divergent Mind* is a signpost to a happier future in which the diversity of human wiring is celebrated."

—Steve Silberman, *New York Times* bestselling author of *NeuroTribes*

"Empowering . . . This important book not only advocates for research and innovation; it demonstrates the power of acceptance, kindness, and the celebration of differences."

—*Booklist*

"An extraordinary, jaw-dropping take on a topic with which many women will identify."

—*Library Journal* (starred review)

For my daughter

Contents

Trust Your Mind

Introduction

In the Arctic Circle, on the archipelago of Svalbard, Norway, a long, narrow rectangular concrete structure, the Svalbard Global Seed Vault, jets out from a snowy mountain range overlooking the Greenland Sea. Inside there are over 1.2 million seeds preserved securely in the vault to ensure their continuity on planet earth in case their species go extinct. The barren, eerily beautiful surrounding landscape is populated by polar bears, who outnumber the human population, and yet manmade creations like the seed vault, the North Pole Expedition Museum, and other exploration sites dot the island. To imagine the place is to sense both desperation and perseverance in the face of harsh weather, as well as optimism and hope about our ability to wonder.

With smaller seed banks located around the world in most countries, the vault is used as a safety depository for other countries, a "backup" in the face of war or natural disaster. The Philippines, Afghanistan, Iraq, and Lebanon, for example, have all faced severe damage to their seed banks; Lebanon had to retrieve seeds from the vault and replant them to spawn new seeds, before redepositing seeds back to Svalbard. The vault is a much-needed global repository for the world's biodiversity.

Now let's say you were to conjure up a distinct vault of your own, a repository of the world's great art, books, and music, similar to a grand library. Let's say it's digital, and with a touch of the screen you can access any important historical work. Your vault is large, with different viewing areas, and you have two or three people working inside simply to help you navigate around. This vault is just for you, not the public, and you revel in the fact that all the world's knowledge is available to you, making you feel a kind of peace, freedom, and satisfaction that you can squeeze out of life all the intellectual juice you want. You even invite a friend or two inside from time to time, just to share your joy with them.

Then one day, you discover that one of your visitors has a disagreement with one of the people who works inside the vault. The argument isn't overly loud or threatening, but voices are slightly raised, and the event makes you look over from another room. Your friend and the worker (let's call them a "librarian") both brush it off as though nothing had happened, but later you learn more.

It turns out that your friend asked to see the music video for their favorite punk band, and the librarian could not show it or would not show it—the reason was not exactly clear. Your friend has seen the video before and knows it exists, and they're perplexed at the librarian's refusal. You are also perplexed because you never gave the librarian instructions to remove anything or hide something. Questions start bouncing around in your mind. Unfortunately, you also discover that many more pieces of significant artistic history were removed without your permission. The questions and confusion turn into hurt and anger. Your precious vault has been violated and "vandalized"—except there's no graffiti; there's simply the awareness that there are gaps where there once was art.

Now imagine an actual physical library somewhere, in a small town in the United States, dutifully serving children, students, adult readers, and families. One day, the director of the library publishes a report about the importance of preserving access to all kinds of ideas, not just those acceptable to one half of the country or the other. A few weeks later, because she mentioned pluralism and the importance of not limiting ideas and knowledge, the director is told she can no longer work at the library, even though she has been its guardian for eleven years. She thought she was doing her job well, worrying about how libraries were increasingly only ordering certain kinds of books and leaving other kinds of books out. But her colleagues didn't like that she wanted to cast such a wide net of information and access to books. They wanted to limit the knowledge they were offering to their community. So, they terminated her position.

This is a true story that happened not only once in very recent memory but that repeats often nowadays in various forms. And of course it's not limited to librarians, but includes actors, television producers, schoolteachers, writers and journalists, professors, and many other professionals engaged in the work of media and communication. It's also happening inside friend groups, families, workplaces, and communities, where a "wrong" remark or comment results in banishment, and contradictory ideas result in stunned faces and emotional shutdown.

Gathering places and human relationships that used to be precious vaults of safety, connection, community, and knowledge sharing now feel increasingly unsafe; that is, with emotions on constant high alert and a widespread inability to regulate our own selves and how we communicate, people now live in fear of saying the wrong thing, because nuanced inquiry and dialogue have all but disappeared. We don't feel comfortable asking questions. We don't trust in the power of conversation anymore. We're scared and don't want to rock the boat. No one speaks up, and everyone stays silent. This is self-silencing.

The Effects of Self-Silencing

Within an entrenched group identity—even under the guise of "belonging," such as to a political party, religious organization, or class—self-censoring often takes place to preserve group cohesion. It makes sense that people shut down parts of themselves, but it's unhealthy and can even be dangerous.

What do you do, for example, when you are caught up in the swell of groupthink—that is, when you are shunned in your social circle for saying something that is not absolutely aligned with widespread opinion or when mobs of people you don't know start attacking you on the internet for a less-than-popular point of view? Groupthink has a swaying effect on human beings, like a wave pulling minds into uniformity without their consent; the current is strong, and its effects are scary.

I'm not just talking about mobs and cancel culture as they relate to Hollywood, celebrities, and other famous figures we see go down in flames publicly. This "self-silencing climate," as I call it, has trickled down to everyday people: you and your neighbors, your coworkers, your friends, your family members. Your communities. It has impacted everyone's ability to have honest, open conversations, our ability to ask curious questions about the world around us, and to find nuanced answers.

Unfortunately, the internet—that wonderful technology meant to connect us—is a major culprit in dividing us. The emergence of the internet in the last decades of the twentieth century initially elicited worldwide excitement about knowledge sharing and bringing people together, but soon after its emergence, especially with the rise of blogs and then social media, scholars and users alike began to feel uneasy about the rather distorted view of reality that might emerge. Hateful comments that once appeared under YouTube videos would soon begin to spread more widely with algorithmic social media. Exciting news such as the rise of female CEOs saw unfettered bullying tearing the women down. Platforms like Facebook and X would soon become places where haters would find other haters, and the victims of those haters would band together, cementing their identity categories and isolating themselves further. It was most often women and minorities at the receiving end of cyberbullying, and they created fierce groups in opposition to unknown anonymous posters. As algorithms became more sophisticated and companies, including news sites, grew to depend more on clicks, viewers were served up repeated content pertaining to their narrow interests or identity categories, which created virtual iron walls around checkboxes like physical appearance.

When a group of people unknowingly limit their thinking to restrictive identity norms or a virtual bubble with narrow information, whether they are the attackers or the victims, the groupthink *can be blinding.* No one is authentically themselves anymore, and the quiet questions only increase. No one knows how to talk and disagree respectfully, and people have no patience for differing viewpoints and opinions. But people also *crave* these very things; they crave real talk and openness, and the freedom to engage confidently and curiously, without fear.

The presence of toxic fear has wide-ranging effects on our overall well-being. Self-silencing is strongly correlated with depression, according to numerous studies carried out in the past twenty years. And with depression and self-silencing come other negative outcomes like loneliness, feelings of alienation, and low self-confidence. The toxic effects show up in workplaces, intimate relationships, friend groups, online forums, political discussions, religious groups, and more. Especially in a culture where we are encouraged to be ourselves and express ourselves as individuals, the feeling inside us when we don't fully express our truth with integrity and in a genuine way can be doubly harmful, because not only are we not being true to ourselves, we are also not living up to a core value that is upheld in our modern-day society.

No matter what stage of life you are in, you have almost certainly observed a widespread societal discomfort with disagreement and a preference for discussing simple topics over nuanced concepts. We are all dealing with the consequences of a world where conversation is constrained by inauthentic parameters of acceptability, and we think according to the group we belong to rather than the conclusions we have drawn through our own reasoning. To move away from groupthink, we need to relearn how to think as individuals, trust our own complex reasoning, and learn how to communicate those thoughts with confidence and forthrightness.

The antidote to self-silencing is not just free speech; it is *free thought*, where one is equipped and empowered to form opinions using critical reasoning. To think critically and communicate confidently are vital skills many of us have lost, or were never taught. And part of being a critical thinker is to acknowledge the reality that there is a vast diversity of thought in the world and that there is beauty in the clash of opinions that differ from our own. For a variety of reasons, from education to religious indoctrination to gender bias, sitting with complexity and nuance and differing opinions is something that many parents, educators, and community leaders simply do not make time for. It is a rare breed of person, family, or community that sits patiently with young inquiring minds to help flesh out ways of thinking that are inquisitive, critical, open, and agile. But we need such thinkers now more than ever. Critical thinking should become a core value for all of us in the coming decades.

My Story

In order to tackle fear and develop courage and critical reasoning, and to wrap our minds around the vast range of viewpoint diversity in the world, we must weave together several overarching ideas, a bridging that has been central to my career. As a journalist chronicling psychology over the past ten years, and with an educational background in political theory and public health, I have always prioritized cross-disciplinary engagement. The subject of much of my work up until this point has been neurodiversity, or "neurological diversity"—the nuanced but often misunderstood concept that diversity of human cognition is valuable. The idea of neurological diversity embraces the myriad ways in which our brains process and respond to the world and encourages respect for diverging viewpoints and perspectives. My first book, *Divergent Mind,* explored why certain neurological traits like attention differences are often overlooked in women and how society can benefit from encouraging those differences to flourish. And although neurodiversity was a relevant topic in the psychology world, I never thought of neurodiversity as being *limited* to psychology. Diversity of thought is something to be applied in every sphere, every arena and field. At its core, the idea of neurodiversity is "heterodox," which refers to embracing diversity of thought and unconventional viewpoints. Being a heterodox thinker has always been a core value of mine, professionally and personally.

I grew up in San Francisco in a single-parent household with three siblings, where our neighbors, extended family, and classmates were majority non-white folks. We were the minority as white kids living in the Black neighborhood of the Fillmore and attending a public Asian American school in the far west foggy avenues of San Francisco's Sunset neighborhood. I was raised among several religious and racial groups in my own large extended family of Catholics, Jews, Bahá'ís, and Muslims. My classmates ranged from unhoused people to first-generation immigrants to troublemakers to high achievers.

Living in the liberal bastion of free speech meant coming of age within a culture that included community health programs, Black Panther solidarity, Deadheads, and more. I am a millennial, so my time was the '90s, but the culture and ethos of the '60s hippie era were passed down to me, and I hold those values dear. At UC Berkeley, I designed my major in political theory and race relations, and just after graduation I worked at the well-known Glide Memorial Health Clinic in the Tenderloin, the epicenter of the drug and housing crisis in San

Francisco. My roots are in staunch left liberalism. I crave—and love—difference.

As a kid growing up in a multi-faith, multi-class, multiracial family in a progressive neighborhood, I had always been drawn to many-sided conversations and was comfortable being surrounded by different views and backgrounds. I have always been a question asker, a sensitive kid who craved real talk—real answers to life's questions—and I was never one to go along with a group. If something doesn't make sense to me, I can easily switch ideas or viewpoints. If something doesn't sit well with me, I have no problem saying "no" or backing away from a situation, conversation, or person.

When I later learned more about my own mind and the neurodiversity framework, I committed to lifting others up and celebrating those differences, not masking them as we are often conditioned to do. However, I soon discovered that groupthink can exist in and permeate any framework, and while I had embraced differences in the way our minds work and knew that I thrived when faced with multiple perspectives, I found that I often felt social pressure to approach broader societal conversations with caution. I started noticing that there were *things I wasn't saying.* I had thoughts I was too afraid to type, questions too afraid to ask—and over time, this gnawed at me. I've always been someone to advocate for being fully seen and heard, and here I was engaging in severe self-silencing, inadvertently isolating myself along the way, especially in the midst of vitriolic behavior I witnessed online from people who I thought valued open discourse. The black-and-white, all-or-nothing ways of thinking I saw across social media seemed to be rewarded with likes and shares, and I didn't understand how people were being pulled into such polarized sides on issues, with so little information or context. I felt inclined to ask questions to get a better, deeper understanding of someone's perspective, but the online climate didn't feel like a welcoming place to do so, and I always opted to do my own silent research instead of utilizing online conversation and dialogue.

I also felt confused, because my actual lived experience didn't match many depictions of community and culture in the media or the news, and I began increasingly meeting other families in real life like mine who embodied unique cross sections of humanity. But no one I encountered seemed to express those perspectives online, in the crowded worlds of social media or mainstream news. I sensed there was a mismatch, and when I started talking to more people about this, I discovered there was fear, apprehension, and self-silencing because there were no welcoming spaces to share about a different, more complex kind of reality. As I delved further into what was happening and saw how our conversations were being drained of nuance and dissenting opinions, I realized that this phenomenon overlapped with the topics to which I'd devoted my first book. While I had previously focused more specifically on cognitive diversity, it turns out viewpoint diversity is its more expansive umbrella, and all of us are at risk of depriving ourselves of the rich diversity of perspectives and opinions in the world when the nuances of life are drained out and remain veiled.

I had been sitting silently with these thoughts for years. I started with the seed of a question about what I felt was happening to our minds, bodies, and mental health as a result of self-silencing in our online world, but once I decided to pursue the topic as my next project, it took mere hours for stories from others to come pouring out. I was not alone. It turns out *we are all masking and holding questions inside.* I soon discovered many other people like myself, who were open to the joy, wonder, challenge, and complexity of hard conversations and critical reasoning. I decided to write my next book for them.

This Book

In this book, I take my background in journalism, psychology, and public health—from my days studying at Harvard and Berkeley to reporting for CNN, the Greater Good Science Center, and elsewhere—and apply these lenses to the urgent problems of isolation, loneliness, and polarization that are worsening under a culture of self-censorship and lack of tolerance for dissent. In addition to telling the tale of our current collective emotional interiority, throughout the book we will meet people who dared to step out of the comfort of groupthink and embraced nuanced and complex thinking more openly and publicly.

Part I of the book presents a tour of groupthink, from its psychological and social origins to its effects in our modern online era, to the extremes we now find ourselves in. Part II guides us through the first steps in escaping groupthink—deciphering our own thoughts, tolerating the discomfort of breaking away, and shifting to a new way of interacting socially, one that embraces healthy friction and debate and doesn't view complexity and connection as mutually exclusive. Part III presents a vision for the future, one in which a society of freethinkers is able to thrive and embrace diversity of thought—online and off.

My aim is to guide you to draw your own conclusions by introducing perspectives from which to view and appraise contemporary groupthink and how it shows up in your families, friendships, classrooms, social media, religious circles, workplaces, news channels, and pop culture. I cannot tell you what to think, nor do I aim to, but I believe I can expose you to things to think about on your journey to being a sharper thinker and conversationalist as the world becomes more complex and polarized.

This book, at its heart, is an exploratory mission through the deep emotional waters that swirl and froth below the noise of our crowded world. Underneath loud arguments—whether online or at home or on political panels—are vulnerable emotions, but those are rarely talked about, and detecting what's below the surface is a rare skill.

I am intimately familiar with the inner turmoil caused by both the backlash of speaking my mind and the anguish of self-silencing—as a public writer, I've had to wade through tricky waters. The courage to sit with discomfort and uncertainty must be developed if we are to commit to staying steadfast and transforming our relationships with others into pillars of fierce strength.

This book is about my exploration and encounters, but also what you can learn about critical reasoning in a noisy world and expressing yourself honestly in the face of resistance and societal pressure. It's somewhat of an outside-in approach: first exploring why, in an increasingly virtual village, we fall into groupthink and cling to rigid identities. Then, looking inward, we'll explore how to sharply decipher our opinions and feelings, independently of friend groups, office politics, religious norms, and cultural trends. Finally, we consider how we can communicate these complex thoughts confidently and cultivate compassionate conversations that hold space for disagreement *and* connection. My hope is that you will find this useful not only in the online world, but also as you move through the physical world—chatting with family members, making parenting choices, or learning how to be a good friend.

Censorship and self-silencing impact us all, in different ways, and are reshaping our lives right under our own noses—or under our thumbs, inside our smartphones, and outward into social norms—and affecting how we talk and relate to one another, how we *treat* one another. We are at a crucial inflection point in our culture, and the way we navigate these treacherous waters will determine the fate of our future and how we feel about one another. We *know* we are complex, layered creatures, but that truth is threatened in the online world, with its excessive focus on hard-edged, polarizing categories and algorithms that funnel us into binary ideologies. This book will penetrate the performative veil of social media and break down the silos that have formed over many years.

Taking on the mission of writing this book was initially compelled by a sense of urgency, but that urgency was then tempered by months and months of careful marination. Our journey on this mission must take a similarly measured approach, knowing the challenges we face. We are hungry for solutions to the quiet frustrations of self-silencing and lack of dialogue, but there's no quick fix, and we need guidance and reassurance about how to reemerge and reengage. This book offers that salve, generating conversations about how to create a healthier climate in which to see and celebrate differences of all kinds, lean into curiosity and openness, and embrace a plethora of perspectives and opinions.

I offer a road map and a space to question together. My own journey with self-silencing has been one of shock, confusion, stillness, and ultimately triumph and empowerment. In discovering people who value the questions and wanderings and complicated layers of life just as much as I do, I feel more comfortable opening myself up to the nuances of hard, pressing issues.

This shift has helped me feel more myself as I engage with the world and stay open, rather than anguishing over the "correct" version of self-expression. For years, I was afraid to poke holes in certain ideas, questions, or opinions, and this book challenged me to live my life freely and openly again—and I hope it does the same for you.

The challenge is not for the faint of heart, but the payoffs are monumental: If one of our goals as human beings is genuine pluralism, there is a much greater chance of that coming about when people know who they are and that having different views is actually supported and celebrated. Imagine a world where the vibrant buzz of divergent ideas leads to connection, rather than a world where connection is contingent on blind conformity and agreement. Diversity of perspective is a global resource to be harnessed, a treasure in need of preservation, and we should all get to experience the joy of sharing ourselves freely, being challenged, and growing beyond what we ever imagined.

Part I

WHERE WE'RE AT

Chapter 1

The Origins of Self-Silencing Culture

In 2022, University of Virginia senior Emma Camp, who is autistic, published an op-ed in the *New York Times* about her and her friends' encounters with mob mentality in their classrooms when they attempted to question certain ideas. She described scenarios in dorm rooms and campus workshops where friends lowered their voices and shut doors behind them for fear of others twisting mild remarks into distorted, controversial statements. For instance, Emma felt it was acceptable for people outside of a given culture to question rituals that endangered lives, in this case, the Indian practice of sati, which is when widows immolate themselves upon their husbands' funeral pyres. It is an ancient tradition not commonly practiced today, but the issue she encountered was not so much about the subject itself, but about her place to comment on it given that it is not her own culture. In an academic context, her impression of college was that students come to grow and learn through disagreement, challenging discussions, and debate, and she was shocked to discover that this is not always the case. In her op-ed, she also referenced a woman who challenged the idea that a superhero film was laudable simply because it portrayed a woman's physical strength; the student thought that more attention should be given to the character's wrestling with internal conflicts, to which her classmates scoffed in resounding disagreement. And while disagreement is perfectly fine, it was odd that the entire class seemingly felt one singular way. Everyone piled onto *one* perspective. "Throughout that semester, I saw similar reactions in response to other students' ideas. I heard fewer classmates speak up. Eventually, our discussions became monotonous echo chambers. Absent rich debate and rigor, we became mired in socially safe ideas." After the op-ed was published, a new mob found her on X, railing against Emma's social conservatism, though she identifies as a left-leaning libertarian. For Emma, it is this lack of nuanced inquiry and dialogue that has felt shocking to her during her young career, but it has only emboldened her dedication to open inquiry and reporting.

Part of her story here is that autistic people are often the first to feel that something is off among groups due to their sensitivity to hypocrisy and inconsistency. When it comes to self-silencing, more and more people who are sensitive are standing up and speaking out. Sensitive folks tend to sense social inconsistencies, hypocrisies, and inaccuracies because many of us pick up on subtleties—like mannerisms, gestures, and linguistic patterns that don't follow expected rules—and we feel "off" as a result, slightly irritated or disturbed. It is actually this sensitivity that makes some of us appear to march to a different drum, not a lack of awareness, as is commonly misunderstood. When scrolling on social media, I sometimes feel literal sensations in my stomach as I browse and watch how people feed off one another. And we often notice when something is "up" in the collective climate. The online world sometimes feels similar to a cultlike, caged environment, which is a sensation that is quite the opposite of what people need on a sensory level. Most of us have somewhat of an "allergy" to going along with a group when it doesn't feel right, and it can feel physically out of alignment to not follow our own senses.

A climate of self-silencing is disturbing to many sensitive people, and we often notice its presence right away. Perhaps this is because we have experience with the downfalls of "masking," which is when people hide parts of themselves to blend in. While some neurodivergent folks who struggle with self-regulation can themselves fall prey to mob mentality, many others resist groupthink because they recognize it as a controlling and arbitrary social expectation to fall in line and mask individual truth in favor of robotic conformity.

You can imagine the tremendous amount of energy required to mask and suppress individual truths—whether it's a diagnosis or beliefs and opinions—over lengths of time. Numerous studies show that depression and anxiety often result, creating a confusing internal mingling of self that struggles with feeling whole, healthy, complete, and accepted. Unfortunately, *these same feelings resulting from self-censorship have begun to spread,* resulting in what I call a "self-silencing culture," the everyperson's equivalent to cancel culture. While cancel culture feeds clickbait-y headlines online, the feeling of self-silencing permeates everyday life, where people feel censored both online and off.

Groupthink: From Helpful to Harmful

It started out innocently enough.

When we zoom out, it's easy to understand the potential social function of conformity and how it begins; in fact, a study out of the Max Planck Institute of Evolutionary Anthropology in Germany showed that conformity starts as early as two years old. In the study, a group of children were tasked with dropping balls into boxes, and if the ball went into one of the particular boxes, they would be rewarded with a chocolate treat. But even after a toddler had completed the exercise correctly and was aware that a certain box produced a treat and the other boxes did not, when they watched their toddler peers drop the ball incorrectly, the first group of successful toddlers would copy the second group, even though that action did not produce the chocolate like the first time.

Outside of toddlerhood, and beyond chocolate, we can imagine how conformity has kept groups and individuals safe throughout time: Don't burn yourself touching fire, don't run too fast near a cliff, show respect to your elders, and so on. Conformity matters in certain cases of literal and existential survival. But it has a dark side, especially as civilizations grow and technology advances. Whispered rumors turn into a witch hunt, and people die as a result of hysteria and lack of critical thinking. Narrow notions of skin color, ethnic identity, social class, and more justify the execution of millions. There is no shortage of examples where conformity is extremely dangerous, no matter the era. In contemporary times, mass media has quickened the pace at which ever-larger numbers of people fall in line to conform. That is perhaps the scariest thought of all. With phones in our pockets and apps that reach millions right under our thumbs, everyone is at risk of being hijacked by outrage and emotions that hinder critical thought and encourage blind conformity.

The Modern Media Machine

It is impossible to understand modern self-silencing culture without first understanding the recent history of modern media. In her book *Bad News*, author Batya Ungar-Sargon outlines the riveting history of journalism in the United States, from neighborhood papers to Fox and CNN to social media. Modern journalism in this country began in the nineteenth century with tiny "penny presses" in working class neighborhoods of New York City. They were meant to capture the everyday lives of ordinary people—and far from information sharing being viewed as a "luxury," people in those neighborhoods desperately wanted information that covered issues important to them.

In the late nineteenth and early twentieth centuries, as New York high society cemented, the demand for presses to cater to *their* needs and interests skyrocketed, thereby creating a playing field of new presses that competed for elite status. Everyone wanted to be seen reading the new social class signifiers, and to be featured in such pages was considered a mark of "making it." Advertisers caught on to this, learning the revenue potential by marketing their products to high-income readers, and they all jumped on the craze. Journalism was no longer aimed toward the working class, and business models continued to develop as such.

Media still very much functions this way, and at some point, through user testing and insights from psychology and marketing, tech leaders realized that the most engaged readers were the ones most vulnerable to outrage and intense emotion, which meant that they could gain the most by catering to that audience. Thus began a shift from information sharing to sensationalizing, profiting off the promotion of stories that fuel hatred and polarization, while suppressing reportage on more complex, nuanced issues. In recent years, multiple reports have come out about biases shaping the *New York Times,* NPR, and TED, for example, where concerns about viewpoint diversity were suppressed in favor of more provocative stories that were ironically deemed more socially safe. Thankfully, these and other outlets have also made recent efforts for more balanced coverage in response to widespread critique.

But the abandonment of nuanced coverage and the lack of encouragement of open conversations has plagued contemporary journalism and catalyzed long-lasting repercussions for our democracy, as well as our ability to authentically connect with one another. And now it is the *vehicle* of information—the internet and social media—that may be our greatest obstacle.

This vehicle that now dominates the sharing of information—fueled by ideals of community and a public square and allowing for endless comments on videos, interviews, opinion pieces, and more—is an amorphous world, like a floating city, and it is now forcing us all to contend with not only deciphering truth from misinformation, but also our own minds and emotions. Reading a print newspaper calmly at home is a vastly different experience from pulling out a phone on a crowded bus and being bombarded with multiple visual streams of information.

Internet Groupthink + Anonymity: A Recipe for Disaster

In the mid-1990s, commentators began sounding the alarm about the risks and dangers posed by the internet of creating a loss of community and a world of strangers. Internet friendships would soon be "convenient, even entertaining, but, lacking both the context and the embodied basis of emotional support, they may be at the cost of more involving relationships," wrote psychologist John A. Teske in a 2002 article for *Zygon: Journal of Religion and Science.*

He continues, "If all thinking is really a kind of conversation, it is never a small challenge to convert it into a medium of pure words, and much of the feeling, the embodiment, and the lived reality behind it is likely to be missed." Now a retired professor in rural Pennsylvania, Teske's writing is some of the only material that has consistently continued to capture the "disembodiment" of this hyper-online era from those early years onward. "Social forces, technological and otherwise, have increasingly eroded our social interconnectedness and even produced psychological fragmentation," he boldly wrote in 2002, ahead of his time.

The internet is the ultimate escape, but what are we hiding from? My take—and my fear—is that people are addicted to the internet because they are deathly afraid of their own physicality, their own ordinariness and mortality. Teske shares this concern. As a result of the internet, he writes, "We can feel less vulnerable, less anxious, perhaps in part because we make less apparent the vulnerabilities of our bodies and our anxieties about the deeper vulnerability of our mortality. . . . The problem is in the denial of physicality, of embodiment, and of the very biology upon which so many of our spiritual capacities depend."

Summing up what would soon define the next twenty years and beyond, he writes, "Unfortunately, and perhaps paradoxically, while electronic communication in its many guises may enlarge our web of actual interdependency, the increasing personal-computer-based use of the Internet is likely to involve a more elaborate construction of our sense of privacy and whole new worlds of personalized, individual interiorization. The risk is that it will produce further isolation and fragmentation, even to the level of internal dissociation."

While many commentators were optimistic about the connectivity and access to information enabled by the internet, others were worried about the social consequences—and both groups were right. Social media and the internet have given the world so much, but they have also created an entire universe of new challenges. The 2001 book *Towards CyberPsychology*, for example, opens with the line, "The diffusion of new communication devices and experiences will soon change our interaction experience." Not only that, but writing the next year, John Teske commented that "there are real issues of information quality on the Internet and an information overload that often results in restricted attention." Reading these predictions and premonitions from two decades ago, I can't help but think, "You have no idea how right you were."

The internet has certainly changed the way we think, but what is perhaps more important to consider is that *it has changed the way we perceive the world and one another.* With some opinions amplified more than others, the result is that we take on a warped view of public sentiment. This kicks off a vicious cycle, in which the less we hear from individuals with differing opinions, the more we are afraid to voice our own, thus perpetuating a skewed sense of what people really think and feel. We often mistakenly think that everyone in our circle views a particular issue the same way, and with that comes the fear of saying something that will lead to condemnation from the crowd. Ioana Kocurová-Giurgiu, a communications consultant in the Czech Republic, writes that cancel culture is "promoting a level of self-censorship that is essentially limiting free speech, thus engaging in a one-sided dialogue mirroring a false reflection of reality that is detrimental to society and its democratic values."

But it's hard to push against the grain when technology and groupthink cement together. Social media and groupthink are inextricably tied together because algorithms have leveraged human psychology in highly effective and addictive ways. The same hard-edged categories of group identification that fuel self-silencing and cancel culture are the very same phenomena fueling media outlets today via clicks and dollars. There is no separating the two: divisive categories are highly lucrative for news outlets because algorithms know what to do with them and who to serve them to, thereby making those posts, videos, and articles go viral. The side effect is that while clickbait fuels media consumption, divisive categories become even more deeply entrenched and those whose views fall into the in-between gray areas are forced to self-silence even more because we believe we exist in a philosophical wasteland. But as we will see, that's a lie, and there are growing numbers of us who stand proudly in the gray.

Group Dissenters and Identity Orphans

Perhaps the most tragic sacrifice in the rise of groupthink is the loss of independent critical thought. The internet likes to funnel us into categories: progressive/conservative, urban/rural, rich/poor. This helps serve the "right" content to the "right" audience. But this strips away the reality that we are multifaceted beings, no matter our individual circumstances.

In truth, we relate to slivers and elements of many well-defined groups and hard-edged categories, but none define all of who we are. We exist somewhere at the frictions and interstitial spaces between what we think of as solid boxes, with walls patiently waiting to combust—seeking, yearning to connect, bridge, merge, re-whole.

Erec Smith is a professor of rhetoric at York College of Pennsylvania and the cofounder of Free Black Thought, a collective of diverse voices pushing back against reductive narratives about Black thought and identity. I've long admired his nuanced writing and sharp thinking, and I respect and appreciate his willingness to continually push back on dominant narratives about race. One morning over Zoom, I wanted to better understand his personal story and how he arrived at being somewhat of a rebel. Has he always been so outspoken?

Where, exactly, did Smith's penchant for nuance and resistance to groupthink come from?

> It developed when I was a kid, at fourteen or fifteen. I was born and raised into a predominantly white neighborhood,

> so they weren't exactly nice about it. I got a lot of heat about it. When it was time to graduate primary school and go to secondary school at a school that was much more diverse, literally 50 percent Black, I was over the moon that I could finally get out and be with like-minded people. But boy was I wrong. They were just as harsh for opposite reasons—they thought I was too white, having been socialized in a predominantly white neighborhood. So that's when I realized these two groups couldn't be more different, and yet they both have in common the desire to humiliate me, the desire to tell me that I am not adequate in some way—either that I'm not white enough or that I'm inauthentically Black.

This is also what first piqued his interest in rhetoric. Although he wouldn't have called it that at the time, he was fascinated that both groups had similar goals but different framing.

The big "it" for Smith has always been the power of free, individual thought: "So I learned then that group affiliation is overrated, mainly because I wasn't allowed to have one. I embraced the individuality and saw the efficacy of it, and only later realized it was the primary tenet of classical liberalism."

Smith went on to complete his doctorate in rhetoric and started teaching. One day, over several emails among others in the field of rhetoric, he began to push back against some of his colleagues' "diversity, equity, inclusion logic": "I pushed back on a keynote address that argued that teaching standard English to students of color was inherently racist, and that the very presence of white professors was a problem." He questioned whether this argument was in the best interest of helping students. "I felt the same way I did when I was fifteen, except that the two groups were combined now. Now the Black and white groups were working together to humiliate me because they're not comfortable with who I am. That response is why I'm here today. I realized that for some people, there is only one way you're allowed to be Black, and both Black and white people will police you." And while some might make the case that we should make space for multiple variations of the English language, Smith's argument and perspective is that there is nothing inherently racist in teaching the standard way.

I ask Smith what his larger goal is given his newfound advocacy around Black thought, diversity, and identity. He shares with me that his goal is to bring wider attention to the fact that there are so many ways to be Black, and that there is no single definition. He is a tireless advocate for the power of debate, deliberation, communication, and discourse—and he sees those things as being vital to any democratic civil society. "I want to put the importance of deliberation and rhetoric at the forefront of people's minds, especially when people think about getting along as a country," he tells me. "A lot of what is going on is an inability to speak across differences, so I think the field of rhetoric and the discipline of rhetoric have a lot to offer." He reiterates how important it is for him to share the wide range of viewpoint diversity within Black America, and how integral the field—and practice—of rhetoric is to that understanding.

For Smith, rhetoric is the "study of translation"—i.e., how to get one's ideas out into the public marketplace of ideas and be effective and persuasive in one's communication. He considers group affiliation an easy way out, that group participation merely alleviates fear and insecurity superficially and temporarily. "Rhetoric is one of those ways to exercise agency outside of one's comfort zone," he says. "It teaches you that you should discern, to the best of your ability, the values and beliefs of audiences—and that necessitates listening and empathy. Most initiatives start with 'How do we all get along?' versus 'How do we know ourselves?'"

I ask Smith his thoughts on the notions of "community" and "belonging." Does he want to abandon these concepts?

> Individuals should be able to choose the groups we're associated with. There are certain things we have in common by default, but that doesn't mean that we're all the same people now. So there is commonality that one can use as "group orientation," but when it comes to practicality and living one's life in everyday reality, we should be able to choose our associations—and that's the point of civil society. So even if you're born into a community, you're an individual with agency—and when you're allowed to exercise that agency, you can choose to leave that community. And it shouldn't be a big deal. So, I believe in community, but I believe in voluntary community and not coerced community.

In the realm of ideas, critical thinking, and rhetoric, we can wander through life's fascinating questions together in a sincere quest. When we try to connect through identity alone, we limit ourselves. For example, when faced with the question of my own identity, how am I to decide what defines me? What is most significant—my lived experience as a woman? My neurodivergence? My work as a journalist? I don't feel as if any of these things is adequate to describe the many forces that have shaped the interior architecture of my mind and viewpoints.

To be clear: I am not arguing for the abandonment of all the critical progress that has been made in advocating for better representation of historically marginalized identities. I am asking us to imagine the removal of entrenched group categorizations to begin with, such that we treat each individual before us with the focused attention, love, respect, and curiosity for the particular nuanced being that they are inherently.

I know there are plenty of others who feel as I do, but if there is no name for a new road or color or mountain, no one knows what to call it. And so it stays unnamed, and too often unspoken, even though it *can* be described. Perhaps we misfits are "subcategories." I like to refer to us as "identity orphans," because inherited categories fail to survive in the face of who we really are.

Maybe you are a "third culture" adult now, or you grew up in the heart of a big city like I did, or were raised on a military base abroad. You are infinitely complex in a world that wants to peg you one way or another. In medicine, there is a term—"subclinical"—for when there are aspects of a diagnosis that fit a person, but they're not quite "over the edge" enough to categorize them firmly into a diagnostic category. It's actually ridiculous because the person is suffering, but just not badly enough to pass the threshold of a clinical diagnosis. As more and more people fall under this category, medicine has started using the term "spectrum" to describe things like autoimmunity, for example (a person falls somewhere on an autoimmunity spectrum even if they do not have an autoimmune disorder by clinical definition). The point is, larger categories with yes/no classification work well for broadly segmenting the population, but they fail at accurately capturing our unique individuality.

When I asked my community of readers to share their thoughts on being dissenters and identity orphans, Amy, an artist in Canada, wrote,

> The problem in our society today as I see it is that we are gravitating towards the extremes of the spectrum and ignoring the reality of our complex and nuanced world, which is the existence of all the array of different shades of gray. As an autistic person, I have a strong "bullshit detector," and I am taken aback from the lack of critical thinking in our "politically correct" Western world. I cannot identify with any one political party, because my views and values are more focused on what's good and effective for most—transparency and honesty instead of partisanship.

There is a massive majority of any group that does not fit the extreme that the media portrays, and one of our biggest fallacies as humans is that we take the extreme for the norm. The media picks up on the most extreme expression of one's group and capitalizes on it with your clicks and dollars, both in the nightly news and in big-budget, high-adrenaline films. Among the people I have met along this "heterodox journey," many would belong to "minority groups," and none of them match the extremes portrayed.

Many heterodox thinkers are gifted, introspective individuals—and many are in distress as a result, because to hold complexity and the complications that come with nuanced thinking is, in some ways, a heavy burden. It's rewarding, to be sure, but it can also be lonely. It is deeply uncomfortable—sad and depleting—to see interwoven layers when others only see flat surfaces. It is isolating to see multiple perspectives in a world where other people only see one.

It takes courage to be your nuanced self in a world that wants to lump you, group you, simplify you. Identity orphans know this, and neurodivergent people know this. It can be very alienating, but when we summon the bravery to stand out from the crowd, we give others like us the chance to discover that we're not as alone as we may feel.

Group dissenters and identity orphans don't take refuge in any label, especially any term that came into being in reaction to the past. We should never be defined by one sliver of ourselves, but rather allowed to emerge in our fullness. That can't happen under conditions of self-censorship.

There is hope, however. I'm beginning to see cracks in the fundamentalism and a shift toward building bridges—lone voices online are beginning to swell together, from authors to activists to podcast hosts and even therapists. I'm hopeful for a shared future that blends the free exchange of ideas with contextual awareness—a historical awareness that no doubt informs "identity," but does not *limit* identity and the "self" in pursuit of conformity.

From college campuses to the online ecosystem, learning how to embrace disagreement is hard, but worth it. We need new models, new examples, new thought leaders. They're starting to appear, but we all need to shift our attention toward them, rather than let ourselves be gripped by outrage and pulled in further by simple talking heads and the torrents of social media. When we reason critically and become discerning, there is hope for our own sense of well-being, as well as for our communities. We must endeavor to become aware of the trappings of groupthink and once we do, we will be equipped to traverse our complicated world with the confidence born of hard-earned individual thought.

Chapter 2

The Effects of Groupthink

The entrenched groupthink we see online today—the almost zombielike alignment of opinion—has real influence offline that impacts our in-person interactions. On an individual level, for the millions of teachers, tech workers, therapists, plumbers, stay-at-home parents, carpenters, doctors, professors, firefighters, nurses, and more, there is a real psychological crisis on our hands in the day-to-day world. We are living in psychologically toxic times where people are afraid to openly question, explore, and debate—things that can ultimately bring people *together*. Without that friction being allowed in the first place, there is no tension to overcome, and so the quiet questions inside people's minds remain stifled. This affects everything from friendship and work to our democracy, family life, and the very intellectual and philosophical traditions that inform our world and that we hold dear.

As a result, we see hypocrisy in politics, friendships formed through blind agreement on ideology instead of trust and understanding of who each individual really is, and folks co-opting the original purpose of "speaking truth to power" into opportunities to air personal conflicts on public platforms.

In many instances of contemporary cancel culture and ensuing mob attacks, the "trigger"—when you take the time to actually listen or read what was said without adopting others' opinions first—is surprisingly mild. Of course there can be serious triggers as well, but in many cases the rise of the mob is powered by a *severe twisting of meanings and taking things out of context.*

Nowhere is the issue of mob mentality, groupthink, and self-silencing more public or hotly contested than on college campuses and schools, where dozens of professors and teachers have lost their jobs due to cancellation, and where new testimonies continue to emerge about the icy aura of self-censorship that haunts dorm rooms and lecture halls alike. There was a Canadian teacher in Toronto who was beloved in the field of education for many years who challenged, very specifically, a comment that a diversity workshop facilitator made that the Canadian education system was as unjust as the American education system. The teacher chimed in to point out that, based on the history of both countries, Canada actually had fairer policies on the whole. He wasn't saying that Canada didn't have *any* problems, but he wanted to point out the nuance to the workshop facilitator. But in response to this mild comment, the workshop facilitator put the teacher on the spot, where she accused him of saying that Canada's education system was fair and had *no* problems at all. There is a recording available of what the teacher said, and he made absolutely no comment about an absence of unfairness but simply said that Canada's system seemed fairer to him compared to the United States, since he had spent time in both countries' educational systems. Then at the second workshop the following week, the facilitator presented the teacher as an example of "resistance" to what the facilitator was trying to teach (about inequities in education), all of which led to the teacher feeling humiliated and robbed of honest dialogue. The teacher ultimately filed for workplace compensation for the mental distress of the distorted communication dynamic and lack of work he experienced as a result, which was granted to him. The report indicated that the conduct was "abusive, egregious and vexatious, and rises to the level of workplace harassment and bullying." However, his reputation never recovered, and he was not welcomed back into the school he had been working for. For over two decades he had been a devoted and widely celebrated principal and educator at different schools, championing alternative learners, but in 2023, he died by suicide, as he never recovered from the mental distress and emotional toll of these events.

Over in Minnesota at Hamline University, a professor of

art history was preparing to show a painting that depicted the Prophet Muhammad, something she knew was acceptable for some Muslims but not all, so she took multiple precautions both in her syllabus and during the online Zoom class to say that the painting would be shown briefly. The image is used in art history classes all over the world, often without warning, but the professor felt precaution was necessary for her students' agency and well-being. Unfortunately, one student was disturbed by the image and confronted the professor after. She had not notified the professor in advance, nor did she leave the Zoom room when it was announced that the image would be shown, instead discussing the issue with the professor afterward and then writing to the school administrators. The professor was alarmed by the conversation with the student, so she notified her department head, who responded by saying, "It sounded like you did everything right. . . . I believe in academic freedom, so you have my support." But the *administrators* felt differently, and ultimately revoked the professor's contract for the following semester. The professor is now suing the university.

The climate of fear over disagreement or misunderstanding affects students as well as professors. As Emma Camp described in her *New York Times* op-ed, even making a casual comment in class can lead to public ostracism. Out of fear that they will be shunned by their peers, students tend to keep quiet, adopting a "better safe than sorry" approach to participation. Not only does this dilute the quality of discussion in classroom settings, but it also takes a toll on the students' individual well-being. A

2019 study in *Social Psychology of Education* showed that self-censorship among college students resulted in sadness, anxiety, anger, poor academic outcomes, poor quality of relationships between teachers and students, and, intriguingly, reduced student autonomy. While many of these effects seem obvious, I find this last feature of particular interest because it highlights the ways in which young minds proceed onward from college essentially on shaky ground, unable to stand on their own in their beliefs; the experience of hiding themselves stunts their growth and autonomy.

The literature on self-silencing and depression goes even further to show links with stress, perfectionism, and ruminating thoughts. University students are particularly vulnerable to a range of poor mental health outcomes due to inexperience and newly granted independence, and they are highly susceptible to the mental gymnastics exacted by theories and ideologies that may end up ultimately causing them to self-silence for fear of "getting it wrong" or "saying the wrong thing." All of these opaque rules and rigid, silent codes of conduct are too taxing at an age that should be defined by exploration, curiosity, and encountering the unknown with openness.

In graduate school in the United States, reports indicate that roughly 50 percent of PhD students eventually disengage with their academic programs—and that means either completely dropping out or taking extended leaves of absence; many cite burnout as the cause. I come from a family of PhDs and can testify to the grueling nature of the academic track, but stories of isolation and loneliness are constantly echoed everywhere, from social media platforms to news articles. What makes the experience so tough?

When I went through undergrad and grad school, we were thoroughly trained to be on high alert for any tiny aspect of a sentence we disagreed with or took issue with, so we could focus intently on it in our essay assignments critiquing the author. We were taught to break apart paragraphs, challenge what we were reading, occasionally discuss in groups, and basically analyze ad nauseam. While careful consideration of ideas is vitally important work, sometimes we lose the plot in the process—that is, if examining in excruciating detail ultimately results in distorting the original meaning of the material, we get lost in a swirl of ideas that lose their ground. As ideas can become untethered, people, too, can become untethered. And whereas engaging in lively constructive feedback might help connect humans to one another, ego and vicious readings of one another instead tear us apart.

As such, the current state of higher education is that academic scholarship grows as professors within a given field or department critique each other's work, publish new work, and go back and forth responding to critique in journals, and this cycle continues as more and more insights gather and build, like a giant tumbleweed or a sandstorm gathering strength. With the same precision students are taught to critique and break *material* apart, academics tear *at each other* and each other's work. This is the culture of academia and can be described as nitpicking on steroids. With every sentence dissected and ultimately imbued with new meaning by rival academics, it's difficult to hold on to the original intent of the author's ideas. At any moment, a writer's thoughts can be picked apart by a rival so as to support a distorted interpretation and bolster a rival argument. Perhaps this is one of many reasons why so many PhD students decide it's too much and quit. The nitpicking nature of academia may have indirectly set the stage for mobbing and self-silencing culture, hindering the very purpose of education and the cultivation of ideas and exploration. Is it any wonder that, outside of academia, we are living in a hellish cycle whereby mob culture silences everyday people and then the more silent people are, the less they speak openly or engage in critical reasoning and conversation?

By creating a culture whereby you earn points for tearing others down, it is impossible to lift up a more celebratory culture where sharp thinking devoid of insults is praised and rewarded. The corrosive nature of academia is much more widespread now beyond college campuses—every year as graduates move out into the world, they take that same cutting ethic with them, because that is what they're taught to do. In spheres as diverse as education, government, technology, therapy, and more, it can sometimes feel as though we're primed to be on high alert and see one another as figures we're supposed to resist or be highly suspicious of.

But academia is certainly not the only culprit, and popular media has functioned in the same way, gathering views, clicks, and dollars, capitalizing upon the extreme or outrageous nature of the content. The combination of a highly but narrowly educated populace and those on the other end of the spectrum who haven't had the privilege of a decent education centered on critical thinking—plus a media that thrives on outrage and class division—has, in large part, contributed to the tense climate we now find ourselves in during everyday interactions at the grocery store, with friends, at home, and online.

Disagreeing ≠ Being Offended ≠ Being Traumatized

What kind of people have we become in the face of fear and an overemphasis on tearing each other down? Are we wired for conflict, or are we behaving in such ways in response to the changes in our media and outside influences?

There is an actual term used to categorize personality traits that appear to make people more easily offended: *proclivity to be offended (PTBO)*, coined by Professor Jeremy B. Bernerth at San Diego State University. In a 2020 article in the *Journal of Business Research*, he argues that PTBO is a "state"—that is, not the product of a single event or interaction, nor is it "moral outrage," but rather a disposition, a "state" someone remains in, where even innocuous occurrences stir up offense. One could argue that the excessive focus on hard-edged labels and intolerance toward disagreement today has created an entire PTBO culture. It's simpatico with self-silencing culture.

Bernerth is interested in the way PTBO affects people at work, specifically their task performance and productivity. If one's attention and mental energy are constantly diverted to managing perceived offenses, such a state would negatively impact their ability to focus, interact with their team, and accomplish projects altogether. Those who are "high in PTBO" are found to have lower performance than their peers who are low in PTBO.

To make his point, Bernerth uses terms like *sportsmanship* and *citizenship behavior*—characteristics that enable a person to focus on the big picture, take things in stride, and not get bogged down by setbacks. "People who experience cognitive interference report dissatisfaction at an inability to become absorbed in key life events," he notes. This is telling and gives us a sense as to the daily toll that a disagreement-stifling culture takes on people. As Bernerth writes, "Individuals who persistently monitor the environment for offensive events prime themselves to view ambiguous organizational actions and decisions as being offensive/unfair."

Shockingly, as Bernerth set out to conduct three studies to conceptualize and test the phenomenon of PTBO, he found that those high in PTBO, contrary to what one might expect, are not the more helpful or friendly coworkers. This is surprising, because one would imagine that being more easily offended may cause someone to be more sensitive and caring toward others. Instead, they may be less *relational* overall.

His work also ties into a concept called *organizational justice*, which refers to employees' perception of fairness within their workplaces. The higher the PTBO, the worse they perceive their organization. His studies find "the proclivity to be offended to customarily innocuous societal events and traditions spills over to employees' perceptions of how the organization treats them." In other words, it's vital that people learn to apply a nuanced lens to everyday interactions, otherwise warped perceptions will negatively impact the health of individuals and organizations.

Some workplaces, organizations, and corporations are indeed explicitly toxic, unjust, or abusive, and it is vital that everyone is trained in sensitive communication, ethics, and fairness. But, Bernerth writes, "Paying close attention to personal interactions and the manner in which organizational policies and decisions are enacted provides a good starting point, but both anecdotal and objective data suggests giving in to those individuals expressing the most outrage is not an advisable strategy."

We need to start parsing out what are simply mundane expectations necessary for humans to accomplish everyday projects together in workplaces versus rules that are genuinely bad and corrosive. Figuring out such a distinction requires critical thinking, nuance, and compromise, because it's rarely the case that everyone in a workplace feels the exact same way about everything. When individuals have strong reactions to opposing viewpoints, does that necessarily mean they are being oppressed or traumatized? In extreme cases, sometimes, sure. But the extent to which everyday interactions are now painted on social media as "abuse" should cause concern and serious reflection.

Angry Avatars and Thought Censorship

The opaque anonymity of the internet makes it ripe for distorted perception and communication, and without contextual awareness in conversation and embodied presence in physical, in-person interactions, we are all now essentially avatars to one another—with algorithms further fueling the fire. As a result, we become discombobulated, fragmented selves managing pieces of our lives and relationships through the medium of social media—and losing our tethers to the physical lives right in front of us. We are churned in the mills of algorithms, folded like waves of cream to produce gelato, whipped up into a product, stamped with an identity, and shipped off to drive culture and society. *These social media platforms are no longer simply virtual. They now manipulate our sense of reality.* They are orchestrators of hierarchies and of history and of our own precious, individual lives.

Perhaps most frighteningly, the confluence of groupthink, self-censorship, and social media has resulted in people censoring what information they allow themselves to be exposed to in the first place. Purdue University law professor R. George Wright has published extensively on this concern, and in a piece appearing in the *Notre Dame Journal of Law, Ethics & Public Policy* titled "Self-Censorship and the Constriction of Thought and Discussion Under Modern Communications Technologies," he takes particular aim at the issue of self-censorship and its potential for serious damage and morale-lowering in communities. To begin, he shares that his concern starts with people selecting what information to let into *their own minds*, let alone what to say. It's no wonder that people feel disconnected and discombobulated; we can never be sure how much people are censoring their own exposure to critical information. "What is distinctive about this form of self-censorship is the at least partly voluntary and systematic constriction and distortion of the flow of potentially vital inputs into one's thinking or speaking. This is not a matter of refusing to express or articulate one's fully formulated beliefs. The main concern is thus not with self-imposed gag orders, but with self-censorship as systematically refusing to access or seriously engage potentially crucial inputs into the formulation and testing of one's thoughts and speech."

In today's world, people are no longer being exposed to diverse thoughts and viewpoints by virtue of social media's algorithms, which means that self-censorship (or, what we could call "thought exposure censorship") is practically built into our modern media economy. We no longer know who or what is real online. And when the identity groups that people are being funneled into online function as reality-shaping bubbles that reinforce narrow conceptions of the self and humanity, the limited information exposure fuels a cycle in which they become more and more detached from reality and a sense of what it means to be human.

The Consequences of Mobbing and Cancel Culture

The swirl of cultural change and social forces carrying us through this moment are hard and confusing, with many people losing the ability to see one another, talk with one another, and hold complexity and nuance in conversation. All of this contributes to widespread division, loneliness, and misunderstanding, which pose very real dangers to our individual psyches in addition to the overall climate of society. If students, professionals, friends, and family members feel that in order to get along they must hide their observations, and that asking questions is unacceptable or results in harmful consequences, people start to feel constrained, caged, anxious, angry, upset, impatient, or even isolated and depressed.

Depression and self-silencing are found to be correlated, and the correlation is higher among people with low self-esteem. Some studies show that depression can be predicted directly by what researchers call "self-concealment." Other studies show that self-silencing in conflict-filled marriages leads to depression via repressed anger and what's known as rejection sensitivity, which is a heightened fear of being rejected. In other words, we're creating a world where people are more likely to be depressed because we're doubling down on a collective culture and way of being together where people silence themselves and feel afraid to speak up.

In the journal *Advances in Political Psychology*, researcher Daniel Bar-Tal writes, "Self-censorship has the potential of being a plague that not only prevents building a better world, but also robs its performer of courage and integrity." Multiple studies show that courage and a sense of hope are crucial for overcoming depression. And so I have to ask: Is the personal growth of individuals all over the world now stunted because we are silencing ourselves in the face of the overbearing and monstrous tidal wave that is social media?

Billions of people are on social media, beholden to "likes" and "shares"—that highly addictive force—where people seek desperate approval. Researchers from Stanford, Harvard, and beyond consistently show that the brain's reward system, memory, and attention are all affected by the addictive nature of social media and the "dopamine loop" that is created between individuals and their devices. Likewise, people are in dire fear of disapproval and being canceled, and afraid to say the wrong thing. It's a classic unhealthy relationship, and it's emblematic of self-silencing. We've just never seen it happening on such a mass scale.

Chapter 3

Vulnerability to Extremism

While pursuing group identity can be a means of seeking shelter, it can serve darker purposes. Although there is much talk of the importance of "belonging" and "community," what one finds in a group is more often temporary, and the idea of "group identity" has severe limitations. After all, one is bound by one's literal skin and body, subject to one's own thoughts and disenchantments. There will always be some degree of separation, even under the illusion of merging, bonding, or togetherness. In fact, feelings of lack of personal significance or existential uncertainty precede not only group identity, but extremism as well.

Extremism can be understood as a kind of unhinged, unrestrained clinging to intense thought, with an almost addictive or obsessive force. It clouds judgment in politics, relationships, science, education, and more; extremism takes to the edge any semblance of an idea and turns thoughts and perspectives into the only truth. And once you learn extremism's inner workings, you begin to see it all around, on all political sides, and in all aspects of daily life. Understanding it offers a counterweight against which you can measure and temper your own inclinations in a healthier way—given the intense group pressures across social media, we are all, in a sense, swimming in extremism and it merely passes for "the norm." But once you learn about extremism—what it looks like and what motivates it—you may recognize it in your own life. As such, it's important to probe further and evaluate the line between a healthy sense of community and an extreme sense of groupthink; fortunately, researchers and social scientists across the world are hard at work unraveling the hidden psychological forces that shape our mindsets and behaviors, and you deserve to know what is being uncovered.

The literature on extremism is extensive, stemming mainly from wide interest in political violence internationally, as well as more recent ideological polarization found in the United States. Surprisingly, from the studies on ex-terrorists that focus on the psychological underpinnings of radicalization, it's not too far of a stretch to say that some of the same psychological processes occur on a smaller scale every day with our neighbors, friends, and colleagues. That is, some of the same needs and ways of thinking can be found across a range of human interactions, from neighbor squabbles to violent terrorism. Intense needs drive intense behaviors, with belonging, meaning, and purpose being prime examples of what drive our behavior in the world.

Psychologists tackle the study of extremism via various theories. What is missing, however, is a broad framework for how *the internet* has created new groups and pathways of radicalization—and I don't mean exposure to early sites like 4chan, as we saw in the 2000s. I mean that people's minds and conceptions of themselves have literally been altered in parallel with the algorithms reinforcing identity. The internet has created vast exposure, which has created widespread uncertainty, and now led to extreme group identification. The virtual world has created new interest groups, and those groups are now active *offline* and creating real change, for both good and bad. The internet has enabled entire new classes of people, organized around *psychographics*—the classification of people according to their attitudes, aspirations, and other psychological criteria.

As leading group identity researcher at Claremont Graduate University, Michael Hogg writes in *Current Directions in Psychological Science*, "Identifying with a group is a powerful way to resolve self-uncertainty. . . . Self-uncertainty places a premium on identity-defining belief systems that are distinctive, unambiguous, all-encompassing, explanatory, and behaviorally prescriptive." That is, in our era of dizzying information onslaught and wide-ranging identity explorations, groups and labels that offer certainty become highly appealing. And it turns out that this kind of research on the psychology of group identity formation is exactly what is needed to help us understand extremism in ourselves and in our world.

A British social psychologist who spent his childhood in South Asia, Hogg later studied in the UK and settled in Southern California, and he now leads several international research initiatives focused on extremism and group identity. He designed and developed uncertainty-identity theory, which is referenced widely in psychological literature, and its definition is just what it sounds like: *Self-uncertainty makes one vulnerable to groups that have strong, clearly defined norms and rules, thus offering the uncertain person a strong sense of identity and self-certainty.* Applying this theory to today, we can see such a phenomenon all around us, as people we may know in our own lives become captive to any number of ideologies and groups that actually start on X, Instagram, TikTok, or Facebook. Current fads and fan bases around beauty trends like face yoga are mild examples, but more serious cults or ideologies that lead to religious fanaticism are another.

Uncertainty-identity theory is "a motivational account of group and intergroup behavior, and social identity phenomena," writes Hogg, "but it can also explain the conditions under which radicalization and extremism arise and the various forms they can take. People strive to reduce uncertainty, especially uncertainties that reflect on, or are directly about, who they are."

He continues:

> Group identification reduces uncertainty because it causes people to internalize a shared identity and associated group

> prototype, which defines and prescribes who one is and how one should behave and describes how one will be perceived and treated by others. However, some groups and identities are better equipped to reduce self-uncertainty—specifically, distinctive groups with clearly defined and prescriptive identities that are relatively unambiguous and consensual. In more extreme circumstances and manifestations, self-uncertainty can motivate a strong preference for and zealous identification with extremist groups—groups that have identities that echo populist ideology and behavior, and associated conspiracy theories and narratives of victimhood, and have strong and directive leaders who can be populist, autocratic and toxic.

The application of Hogg's theory to our discussion of self-silencing is rather obvious, and I hope illuminating. To put it plainly, when someone does not have a strong sense of self, they are more vulnerable to any kind of group identity, and then the group identification simultaneously makes one more likely to self-censor. It becomes an unhealthy cycle and requires self-awareness and a strong emotional backbone to stay alert, grounded, and true to oneself in the midst of group pressures to conform.

When Needs Compete

Another route to extreme group identity is that of the competition of one's internal needs. We all have needs for safety, connection, shelter, and meaning, and in some people certain needs get crowded out by others, leading to extremism. In a 2018 paper in *Cognition* on the cognitive processes of extremism, distinguished University of Maryland professor Arie Kruglanski and colleagues lay out clear processes of how needs compete. They write, "In the case of violent extremism, the dominant need in question is the quest for personal significance and the liberated behavior is aggression employed as means to the attainment of significance." Kruglanski and colleagues theorize that the winning need then leads to extremist action through a straightforward sequence where someone encounters information, their awareness of an issue increases, attention becomes narrowly focused, and other needs and goals are crowded out.

"Specifically, when the individual's need for significance becomes dominant, it directs or tunes her or his attention to goal-relevant constructs. And it concomitantly draws attention away from other concerns such as one's family, safety, or physical health." In one of their interviews with Sri Lankan suicide squads, a former participant told them that when volunteers are screened, they are invited to a waiting room first and are only accepted to the squad when, during discussions in the adjacent room, they reveal that they are so engrossed that they recall very few details about what the other room had been like. If someone remembers all the details, they are not accepted. Engrossment in the mission is a requirement.

In a chapter appearing in *Social Psychology: Handbook of Basic Principles*, Kruglanski and colleagues write,

> In a state of moderation, basic needs constrain one another so that people tend to avoid behaviors that serve some needs but frustrate others. For instance, an individual may decline a prestigious job offer that would best fulfill her strivings for personal achievement, if accepting that position required a relocation that harmed her ability to manage important social relationships. Similarly, one's need to be respected and admired might be served by engaging in dangerous physical exploits and daredevil adventures. However, concerns for safety and comfort may constrain the risks one may be willing to tolerate and may curb one's enthusiasm about dangerous undertakings. . . . We propose that extremism occurs when a given need acquires such intensity that it dominates and overshadows other basic concerns.

This idea explains how the temptation of belonging may entice someone to pay such close attention to their gender or mental health or race or disability or other feature that their entire being becomes about that one aspect, to the neglect of the rest of who they are. As Kruglanski et al. write, "Obsessive passion pertains to the case wherein an individual obsessively strives toward the satisfaction of a given concern, leaving little mental resources for other concerns."

If the algorithms love your constant posting about depression or gender dysphoria, and you are rewarded with likes and shares, you are going to keep doing it, propelling you further and further down those rabbit holes, like an addiction, and you become a product of the algorithms—essentially, you unintentionally display some of the very traits of an extremist, out of touch with other aspects of *yourself.* I'm not saying that people online don't legitimately experience some components of their affiliated identity groups, but the way it becomes all-consuming is oftentimes a function of loneliness and wanting to belong. This desire to belong doesn't make someone a bad person—it simply makes them human—but our task is to find constructive avenues toward belonging that don't require conformity to a group or an algorithm.

Entitativity and Uncertainty: What Makes Groups Sticky

Beyond the desire for belonging, what is it that makes a person drawn to groups and how do they get stuck there? Michael Hogg writes about "entitativity"—that is, what makes groups "groupy," including norms and rules. In any group you will observe the spoken or unspoken dynamics at work that serve to reinforce certain behaviors and discourage others. And in fact, related to entitativity is the concept of "prototype." The "prototypical person" is the person who personifies what the group is all about, against which members measure themselves and their behaviors. Such individuals are usually obvious in a religious or fraternity setting, for example.

Restrictive norms and rules can reinforce group conformity, further self-silencing, and lead to the loss of individuality. In his PhD dissertation, Hogg advisee Zachary Hohman writes,

> After a group becomes psychologically salient, people no longer view themselves and others in idiosyncratic or interpersonal terms, but rather in terms of their group identities and associated group norms. That is, they become depersonalized and lose their personal identity for their social identity. . . . A consequence of depersonalization is that people are assumed to fit and behave in accordance with their group's prototype. Once a person is depersonalized, we no longer see them as a unique individual; rather, they are viewed through the lens of their group's prototype and evaluated in comparison to that prototype. We not only depersonalize other people but ourselves as well. We no longer think of ourselves in terms of individual characteristics, but in terms of our group's prototype and how well we fit the prototype.

As members of a group, sometimes people are not fully aware they are self-silencing; they may have an inkling of a feeling, but not outright identify that they are not speaking up, likely because the need to belong is dominant. Hogg and colleagues find that the more uncertain an individual is about themselves, the more they gravitate to groups with firm norms, rules, and customs that don't allow for dissent.

Perhaps the lesson or takeaway is to be aware of the pull of groups and to simply choose wisely, but, of course, limiting one's involvement only to perfectly aligned groups is not always possible. Everybody needs a certain amount of community and shared identity. It's only when it becomes unknowingly all-encompassing that it poses a risk, as we are now seeing in the era of social media–induced mass group identification. As Hogg and colleagues write, "When feeling uncertain about themselves in a particular context, people prefer to identify with, and identify more strongly with, groups that are more distinctive, more clearly structured, and associated with clearer prototypes. Such high entitativity groups may be more effective at reducing self-conceptual uncertainty, and consequently people would be more likely to identify with them."

High entitativity groups are often easily identifiable: Cheerleading teams, fraternity brothers, and adventure groups like mountain trekkers and river rafting enthusiasts might exude a certain "groupy" energy with similar clothing styles, body language, gestures, or vocabulary. But this same "groupy" energy finds its way into smaller groups of friends, online forums, school committees, and more. And the extent to which these groups become problematic depends largely on the individuals and their own levels of self-uncertainty. The more uncertain a person is, the more fanatically devoted to the group they become; Hogg calls such a person an "entrepreneur of entitativity."

Crisis can also play a role; societal crises, just as much as an individual's own life crises, can often catalyze a person to work "diligently to perceptually, rhetorically, and actually increase their group's entitativity." And it is this same diligence that can enmesh people in extreme, violent groups like terrorist groups. War, natural disasters, family abuse, and other circumstances produce widespread existential and individual uncertainty, and Hogg and colleagues argue that "extreme societal uncertainty may tighten the iron grip of ideology and spawn orthodoxy and extremism via social identification [with a group]."

Unfortunately, most of us are now wading in extreme ideological and political convictions fueled by the internet, and sometimes we don't even know we are drowning. Some people become disillusioned and slowly wake up and realize they live in an ideological bubble, but this can take years. By understanding the forces at play in human nature and group psychology, we can retain a sense of clarity and agency. It can be lonely once the fog clears, but we are all better off for a more honest assessment of reality and where we stand within it, and most important, knowing how to more genuinely relate to other human beings as a result of our newfound insights and understanding.

If people do not strive to fully explore and discover how they can make their way through the world in more independent ways, then they "inhabit polarized identity silos, are drawn to populist ideologies and leadership, and find conspiracy theories and narratives of victimhood attractive," Hogg writes in a 2023 book chapter coauthored with social psychologist Amber Gaffney. "Group identification is so effective at reducing self-uncertainty because it provides us with a sense of who we are that prescribes what we should think, feel and do, and it reduces uncertainty about how others, both ingroup and outgroup members, will behave and about how social interactions will unfold. Identification also provides consensual validation of our worldview and sense of self, which further reduces uncertainty."

But what are the psychological features of someone who is so uncertain about themselves and thus drawn to highly entitative groups? Hogg and Gaffney write that a person can feel uncertain about their own "individual attributes" or who they are in relation to "specific other people," but that it's "much more difficult to resolve uncertainty that pervades the entire self-concept—you effectively have nowhere to turn to feel generally more certain about who you are." They continue, "Self-uncertainty can sometimes be experienced as overwhelming and almost impossible to resolve," and they say that this most often happens under three circumstances, the first being that someone has too simple of a self-concept. That is, "they have few distinct identities and those identities they do have overlap so substantially that they are in effect one identity." In other words, they lack the varied exposures and experiences that might help round out their worldview and help them think in more well-rounded and independent ways.

We might thus conclude that high self-uncertainty leads to lower levels of critical thinking. Imagine a person raised somewhat isolated whose limited roles all overlap—for example, someone with few distinct identities might be a person living in the same town where they grew up, working for the same family business they grew up in, and married to someone they've known since grade school. When they leave that nest, they may experience high self-uncertainty because they have not previously been exposed to such different circumstances that would challenge their worldview.

The second circumstance that contributes to high self-uncertainty is when there is "identity overlap uncertainty," such that uncertainty in one area "rapidly metastasizes to affect one's entire sense of self," which describes the above-imagined scenario of difficulty leaving the nest.

Finally, people can feel they don't have the adequate emotional, material, cognitive, or social resources to resolve their uncertainty, and so they experience "an irresolvable and anxiety-ridden threat rather than an easily resolved and exciting challenge," which might happen for the above-referenced person who is first venturing out and experiences a kind of existential crisis and uncertainty in the face of all that is challenging their worldview.

What does this mean for all of us? If uncertainty is inevitable, how do we face it in a way that doesn't make us vulnerable to losing ourselves to the lure of groupthink? Hogg delivers a reframe that I think is helpful: "If one feels one has the resources to resolve the uncertainty, it can be an exhilarating challenge to be confronted—it is exciting and makes us feel edgy and alive and delivers us a sense of satisfaction and mastery when we resolve it. If one feels one does not have the resources to resolve the uncertainty, it can be anxiety provoking and threatening, making us feel helpless and unable to predict or control our world and what will happen to us." To me, this points to the very real need to pivot one's focus during times of uncertainty toward building a firm grounding for your life—from finances to social connections to simple and affordable physical well-being strategies like taking walks. This "taking charge" behavior is especially a necessary pivot for the many sensitive, curious, neurodivergent readers I've interacted with throughout my career for whom creating and implementing logistical frameworks presents a challenge.

As Hogg and Gaffney write,

> Change and the prospect of change almost inevitably create a sense of uncertainty. Change often makes people question their well-established and often habitual understanding of themselves and the social and physical world in which they live. People feel they are no longer able to make reliable predictions and therefore plan adaptive actions. There is a loss of sense of mastery over one's ability to navigate their world. Change and uncertainty are ubiquitous and intrinsic features of the human condition—they cannot be completely avoided. However, people can and do strive to reduce uncertainty. How they do this, and their success in doing so, depends on how strong and enduring the uncertainty is, what its primary focus and origin is, the extent to which it pervades many aspects of a person's life, and on the resources and abilities that people believe they have to resolve the uncertainty.

Escaping Extremism

The research on people who leave extremist groups, referred to as "exiters" or "disengagers," offers interesting anecdotes about how to break the chains of groupthink. According to researcher Anja Dalgaard-Nielsen, who was head of security and intelligence in Denmark, there are three main reasons individuals exit from extremist terrorist groups: doubt, leadership failure, and a change in personal circumstances.

In the case of doubt, people slowly or somewhat shockingly become disillusioned with the "us versus them" narrative in extremist environments and realize that other points of view are valid, thus crumbling the absolutist devotion. "To some exiters the loss of faith appears to be a gradual process. To others it happens due to one eye-opening and dramatic experience," writes Dalgaard-Nielsen.

One avenue for doubt—and this has far-reaching implications for bridging divides and overcoming self-silencing—is that a loved one will enter the life of an extremist, forcing them to reconsider many of their judgments about other human beings. This could be a dear friend, romantic partner, mentor, or other individual. "When this happens, a central notion in militant narratives across different forms of extremism comes under pressure: the division of the world into us and them where we are good and just and they are evil, devious and murderous," writes Dalgaard-Nielsen. "A number of militant Islamists and former left-wing extremists seem to have exited once they gained a perspective on the militant narrative and realized that the reality was a good deal more complex than what the militant narrative postulated."

In the context of self-silencing, the second reason for extremist exiting—leadership failure—is also pertinent. "Some tell of gradually losing the sense of attachment and of the fatigue resulting from constantly having one's level of commitment questioned," she writes, adding that group bickering and betrayal also trigger exits. There is a feeling in the air of not being able to be oneself without constantly monitoring oneself. You may recognize this as a form of "people pleasing."

Finally, when a person's life changes in some way, an exit often occurs. Dalgaard-Nielsen writes that these are often conditions like "burnout, frontline fatigue, growing older, missing loved ones, longing for a normal life, or feeling guilty about the impact of one's extremism on friends and family." Growing older is a common factor in exiting, for example, particularly once a person enters their thirties and generally transitions to higher levels of adult responsibility related to family or work.

The idea of getting pulled into an extremist group or mindset feels a bit . . . extreme, I know. But it can apply on a subtle level to many areas of our lives. So if you find yourself concerned about getting too sucked into one news channel or your social media feed seems to be serving up one narrow point of view, it may be a good idea to know how to pull yourself out of the vortex so you have a clearer, more balanced mind on a daily basis.

Finding a Middle Ground

Esteemed social psychologist Joe Forgas escaped Soviet-controlled Communist Hungary in 1969 at the age of twenty-two by hiding in the trunk of a car of an American who was on his way to Salzburg, Austria. Forgas is now a professor in Australia, and the themes of free speech and liberty have special meaning for him.

He tells me,

> The values of liberty, universal humanism, tolerance, and individualism have been very important to me ever since. Unlike many people who are born into a liberal democracy and take these values for granted, I had to make a conscious, and rather dangerous, decision to seek a new life in a liberal democratic society. As a consequence, I have become more sensitive than most to infringements and limitations of individual liberty and the recent spread of oppressive, collectivist, tribal, and identitarian ideologies and movements throughout the world, by both left-wing and right-wing populist movements. I think individuals and societies must make a determined effort to uphold the enlightenment values that made Western civilization the most successful civilization in human history. This is especially important because human nature as documented by evolutionary psychologists is essentially collectivist and tribal, and as a result all too easily exploited by populist leaders and tribal propaganda.

I'm particularly interested in what Forgas thinks we can actually do about the extremism of today, given his background. And, as a psychology professor, I wonder what he thinks the individual's role is in combating extremism within their own mind. "Experimental social psychology conclusively shows that human beings display a fundamental tendency to behave in ways that serve the purpose of group integration and group survival rather than the rational discovery of reality," he says.

"Human thinking is similarly characterized by confirmation bias, discounting of information that is inconsistent with existing belief, overemphasis of unreliable anecdotal information, simplification, and categorization—these cognitive tendencies again promote the creation and maintenance of consensual beliefs rather than the rational discovery of truth." So, along those lines, he suggests it requires conscious effort to acknowledge bias and then make an effort to keep one's mind open and affirm "values of free speech and the open exchange of ideas, despite our natural tendencies to maintain simple, certain but often incorrect belief systems shared by our ingroup."

At the same time, he tells me,

> The price we all pay for liberty and individualism is the potential loss of a sense of belonging, often resulting in alienation and isolation. The search for identity, significance, and belonging is very common, and of course, is most effectively satisfied by finding meaningful personal relationships, social contacts, friendships, voluntary group affiliations, and social engagement.

> But these are very difficult tasks, and people's need for certainty and identity can be easily exploited by tribal political movements emphasizing group conflict, offering meaning, simplicity, certainty, moral superiority, and belonging to their adherents.

Forgas essentially believes in, and relies on, the power of the individual, supported by political structures and cultures such as the US Constitution that would keep power and bias in check. We know it's not always perfect, but he believes that what Western liberal democracy has accomplished is the most successful so far in protecting individual freedoms, and he is cautious about the extremism of both the right and the left.

Similar to Professor Forgas's views, I came across compelling research on extremism by the researcher Catalina Kopetz, who trained at University of Maryland with the distinguished professor Arie Kruglanski mentioned earlier—and like Joe Forgas, Kopetz, too, was born under an oppressive regime, but inside Hungary's neighbor, Romania. She is now a tenured professor at Wayne State University in Michigan. I begin our video call by asking her how we might make free speech a more dominant "need" for a person. I'm interested in helping people navigate censorship and self-silencing and want to see improvements reverberate throughout society, so what would make a person choose free speech over the need to conform? "There is nothing unique to the need for free speech," she tells me. "I think it goes back to feeling significant and like you matter. You simply accomplish that through making sure that your voice is heard."

"I think that for a lot of people, the need for free speech is a means to feeling significant, that they matter, that they have something to say, or that they have an impact or control over the environment." In other words, for some people, free expression and free speech are the vehicle to feeling more alive, in control, a sense of agency, and significant, crowding out other needs.

Kopetz tells me that based on research on motivation and goal pursuit, which is her specialty, when there is one single goal and one primary need that work well together for a person, that connection becomes very strong—to the point where the goal and the need "fuse" with each other. If people feel like they don't have a voice and that their significance is threatened, she says, then free expression becomes a way to deal with that lack, and the need to speak and be heard becomes overwhelming. It's as though "nothing else matters," as she puts it.

Kopetz tells me about her origins, about her journey from Communist-ruled Romania to France and then the United States, realizing her own motivations and abilities at each step. "When I started my undergrad in Romania, I started right after the fall of the Communist regime after twenty years of a ban on psychology. Ceaușescu hated psychologists because of what they might reveal, so he banned psychology from colleges. They started the psychology programs in the '90s and I was one of the first generations of psychology majors."

Later, when she was in France, she studied under Arie Kruglanski, and their interests were a strong match. He encouraged her to try studying in the US, which she hadn't considered previously, but she wanted to take on the challenge. When she finished her PhD, she wanted to better understand how motivations and goal pursuits played out in applied settings, in the "real world," so she first studied populations who struggled with addiction. "They taught me so much," she says.

I ask her how her academic interests might apply to today—in the extremist environments of social media. Does she think about or pay attention to what's happening online and in our political divides?

"I do," she tells me. "A lot."

"I feel like we've lost any sort of connection with each other, like we're each in our own bubble and expose ourselves exclusively to what is relevant to the bubble and nothing else."

"When you think about extremism—as well as balance—you get balance when there are multiple things that are important to you at the same time, and they require compromise." Remember, Kopetz's specialty is *motivation* and *goal pursuit,* so her language is all about how people manage constraints and prioritization.

"When we are face to face," she says, "forced to interact with each other, you are constrained and you see others react immediately, whereas in the virtual environment you don't have that feedback. You're not forced to be exposed to anything else—and that affords extremism."

"There are no constraints," she reiterates.

Constraints and balance essentially prevent extremism—and social media lacks both. Kopetz thinks social media drives extremes because people are not forced to balance the constraints of real-world, in-person interactions—managing gestures, humor, hurt feelings, body language, and all the other factors that go into daily, mundane interactions.

"Facebook and other social media sites are the worst things to happen to humanity," she adds, recalling when she first signed up for Facebook in 2008 and then quickly deleted it once she realized what it was doing to the mind. When people would hear her express her concerns and then tell her that it helps connect people, she would simply tell them, "These are not real connections."

Her biggest concern is her graduate students. She feels responsible for their careers, but they're growing up in virtual environments that no longer prioritize science, but rather ideology. She also tells me that what does come out of the field is "vulgarized," in her words, and that those who vulgarize get the awards and grants. And then younger PhD students want to be like those people, out in the media, and no one is taking their time anymore, slowly moving through research. "Our goal is to please the crowd instead of being scientists," she says.

"I hope, somehow, something wakes us up."

Part II

BREAKING AWAY

Chapter 4

The Strength to Dissent

Does it feel to you like we've forgotten the joy of dissent, the kind of freewheeling "brainstorming" and thinking out loud that once characterized rowdy, robust university classrooms, where students challenged not only each other, but the professor as well? I'm grateful I had the privilege to experience this kind of environment in college, as well as in my own family dinner table conversations—and even among my friends. Dissent doesn't have to be scary; in fact, it's more like a party.

Unfortunately, we've all collectively gotten ourselves into

a dark, opposite place, where our interactions feel stale, scary, dry, and limited in scope. It's no wonder that banter no longer feels like a party: We are so siloed and isolated that to speak up now feels like *initiating a war*, and we tremble at the thought of merely asking a question. And while it is easy to feel dismayed about the state of discourse, especially online, having platforms for free speech and disagreement is still something to be grateful for. Preserving spaces for dissent should be a global priority.

Not only does research back up the value of dissent, it actually shows that even *within* well-defined groups, *dissenters can be welcomed and appreciated rather than ostracized*. For example, having dedicated time set aside to discuss diverging opinions at school, work, or places of worship can go a long way in building trust. So our work is to inch our way out of this dark place and remember—or even call up images of our own families, favorite films, memories of college life, and whatever else it takes—to find joy in dissent. We can use these memories and examples as inspiration and motivation to do what it takes to get back to that rowdy, energizing discourse and exchange of ideas.

And simultaneously, it's important to acknowledge that leaving behind the stale, quiet "safety" of echo chambers can be difficult. Self-silencing can feel safe, but suffocating, and with the courage to dissent can also come sadness and existential questions. From sports teams and schools to friend groups, churches, and political affiliations, any kind of pivot away from group ideology is difficult.

Losing My Religion

An athlete and mother, Jade went from Evangelical to Orthodox and then entirely away from religion a decade ago. This was one of the most difficult transitions of her life, and she still questions it because of the impact it had on her social support network. She lost her marriage and the closeness with her family. When she tried to join atheist groups, she found the same extremism she observed in religious circles. "I briefly joined some atheist groups . . . but they seemed like the other side of the same coin to me—so sure of everything and so tribal—two things I disavowed when I left the church," she tells me. "I just don't believe it, and once you are out, none of it makes sense at all." At the same time, she says, "But if I'd known how much I'd lose—my sense of identity and belonging and the sense that others thought I was a good and decent person—I might have stayed and quietly quit rather than having made a grand exit."

The term used in religious contexts when one leaves their faith is *deconversion*, and it's a useful concept to explore. *Deconversion* conjures images of casting oneself away—into a liminal, empty space. When one leaves something behind, what is it that they are then joining into? Does that space become ripe for reconversion of some kind? What does belonging offer, anyway? What are the potential psychological considerations of leaving groups, joining new ones, or staying away altogether?

Another helpful term to describe the process and aftereffects of leaving religion is *disenchantment*. According to researcher E. Marshall Brooks, many ex-Mormons experience a "loss of personal identity, debilitating bouts of loneliness and regret, and symptoms akin to clinically defined episodes of depression and anxiety." He goes on to describe presentations of "(dis)embodiment, depersonalization, hyper-reflexivity, and the loss of self-affection among ex-Mormons."

Deconversion and disenchantment are difficult to study, and so far have not been taken up extensively by researchers. As Brooks writes, "Religious disenchantment lacks the very kinds of culturally normative, socially patterned expressions and behaviors that researchers can easily track and describe. Because of this, disenchantment is easily misrecognized/misidentified." This statement sounds eerily similar to what I found in researching autistic "masking" and camouflaging: Hiding a significant part of oneself creates confusion not only for the individual, but also for any potential support system surrounding that person; the lack of clarity often leads to "misdiagnosis," just as Brooks references misidentification here, with disenchantment often looking like general depression or anxiety. It is the phenomenon of hiding some kind of deep truth that is so difficult to ascertain within a research setting until after the fact, when what was hidden often explodes to the surface after a crisis.

In the pages of *The Atlantic*, reporter Jon Fortenbury has taken up the subject of what it feels like to leave religion and has written that "Many who leave religion in America become isolated from their former communities, which can make them anxious, depressed, or even suicidal. Others feel liberated. No deconversion story is the same, but many who leave behind strongly held religious beliefs can see an impact on their health."

There is even a 2010 study showing that only approximately 20 percent of people who've recently left religion can be categorized as in "excellent health," compared to 40 percent who are still active in close-knit religious groups, presumably because the *ease and familiarity of religious belonging* shields people from stress and, to some extent, from the tension and noise of conflicting viewpoints. Tribalism is powerful for the mind and body. But that doesn't mean you should abandon your critical viewpoints for a state of well-being that is removed from (your) reality.

Psychologist Darrel Ray, author and founder of Recovering from Religion, says that his patients typically take two to three years to bounce back from the depression of leaving their church. There is a kind of disillusionment that happens, along with learning to view the world through a new lens, away from former ideals. One could say the same of leaving the extreme left or right, or any other association that we once identified with. There is pain in leaving one's group—the sense of community, belonging, and certainty about the world is lost.

From Groupthink to Freethinking

Stepping away from any kind of groupthink or ideology is going to catalyze a range of emotional responses, including shock, depression, lethargy, relief, confusion, and grief. And anyone who has worked hard to push through the pressure of self-silencing knows that the goal of individual, self-actualized liberation becomes like a burning light in some distant future that one walks toward, through the winds and storms of intense pushback. It is vital that we look at the emotional interiority of the process of overcoming self-silencing and breaking away, and to do so we must tackle various angles, as research on this complex process is limited.

Identity, after all, is a complex web of ideas, experiences, and relational interactions, and when doubt or critical thought begins to surface, there is an existential challenge to the person that is difficult to reconcile and can thus produce depressive symptoms, anxiety, or general angst. When a person remains in such a state, especially engaged in self-silencing over a long period of time, the risk of severe depression increases. It is often the critical thinkers—the millions of people out there who think deeply about any given group ideology, from school to faith to politics to sports—who are bright and want to openly challenge dogma, but, faced with the mental, social, and emotional hurdles, don't. It is too scary to speak out, or perhaps one's entire network of friends and family revolves around a shared ideology, or a person has had a set of beliefs so psychologically ingrained in them that attempting to exit feels morally wrong.

I've heard from many people who left behind group affiliations and identities that took time to shed, ranging from teachers and therapists to athletes, pastors, librarians, students, and more. Denise decided to step away from Waldorf, an educational approach with a formal framework around training children in nature, after teaching within the Waldorf educational system for ten years and having attended a Waldorf school as a child. It is beloved by many, but she chose to leave it when it no longer felt right. However, this personal decision had a ripple effect of consequences. "My choice to leave also meant I basically was cut off by the entire Waldorf community, which had been a home for me since I was a kid and a fundamental building block of my identity," Denise wrote to tell me. "There is a lot I miss and still value about Waldorf education, but the way I was treated when I began to question some of the philosophical underpinnings of the schools and during my subsequent departure has resulted in a great deal of soul-searching and questioning my perception of my childhood and the world."

I also heard from a former conservative therapist in Texas named Jamie. "My dad is a well-known Republican district judge in my small hometown, so identifying as liberal was a really difficult decision with lots of social repercussions in my community," she says. "I am a therapist based in Austin, Texas, and over the last few years I have slowly but surely made a complete exit from Evangelical Christianity." Previously, Jamie says, she was "all in." She got married at twenty-two, did mission trips and "all the church things," she says. "When I started grad school to become a social worker, my views of politics were challenged by new perspectives I had never considered before. I first wrestled with my political identity, having grown up in Evangelical Christian communities that were also very conservative. . . . For a while I tried to be a liberal Evangelical Christian, but over the last couple of years I have revisited my religious beliefs and made the decision that agnosticism aligns with my values and beliefs the best." Having found greater alignment, people like Jamie who dedicate years towards questioning and critical thinking can eventually find a greater sense of peace and authenticity, no matter what they decide.

Another woman, Willow, grew up in a cult where women don't cut their hair, use makeup, or wear pants, and no necklines are allowed below the collarbone. She explained,

> Thankfully, my dad, my main parent, left the cult [when I was] a teenager. I wasn't raised nearly as [strictly as other members], but there was still a lot of the stigma there. Purity culture was heavily pushed, and I wasn't allowed to do things that many of my peers regularly did (I didn't read *Harry Potter* until I was an adult—witchcraft and all that). I struggled with anxiety and depression heavily in high school. Now I know that I had undiagnosed ADHD, but at the time [my symptoms were] just seen as an attention grab. Everyone treated me either as "crazy" or "looking for attention." There was no one trying to look below the surface to see how much I was struggling. It felt, and sometimes still feels, like I'm fighting to keep my head above water.

Willow later moved out of her home state and met her husband at age eighteen, and then they moved to Alaska. "At first, I was terrified of the isolation, but it was one of the best things for me mentally. I was able to step away from my overbearing family and form my own opinions. I walked away from Christianity and conservative Republicanism and have never looked back." She tells me that leaving the tight-knit groups of her youth was deeply isolating, and she still feels like an outsider, "like peering through a window," as she describes it. Unfortunately, she feels like she has to "shove [her] opinions and true self down around them, masking to the extreme," but she ultimately feels at peace with her decisions, though she continues to miss the feeling of community and unconditional love she experienced in the cult, even if it was, in fact, conditional.

These are difficult life transitions, and real vulnerability is required to walk this path. Of course, liberation from groupthink can also greatly improve mood and quality of life. A small study of twenty-four exiters from Christian fundamentalism, for example, found that "freedom from religious conformity, new secular relationships with mutual emotional exchanges, an enhanced sense of autonomy, and personal freedom may have contributed to their greater well-being." As the saying goes, nothing worth having comes easy. But the reward that follows the difficult escape from groupthink and the more empowered sense of self-reliance that comes with leaving a community that once provided a false sense of security is worth the challenge. There is joy on the other side of groupthink.

The True Purpose of Dissent

Jolanda Jetten is a Dutch social psychologist at the University of Queensland in Australia who studies social identity and group dynamics. She also studies dissent, because so much social science research has focused on conformity. For example, she points out that researchers often conceptualize dissent as lack of loyalty, when in fact challenging group norms often implies *deep concern for the longevity of a group's value system.* "Group members may dissent because they care for the group and are concerned about the course of action that other group members are taking," she writes with coauthor Matthew Hornsey. "Dissent is then motivated by an attempt to change group norms for the better, a phenomenon that has been variously described as 'constructive deviance' or 'constructive patriotism.' "

One could say that the large group of heterodox thinkers and writers emerging today have strong pride in being human or in being freethinking individuals. That is their overarching value, and they are what social science researchers call "high identifiers." That is, they speak up because they care. They dissent because they care. And they all have a stake and all care about the future of intellectual life. As such, Jetten and Hornsey write, "highly identified group members dissent because they care about the group. In other words, their dissent is in the service of the group, aimed at changing group norms that they perceive as detrimental."

But sadly, dissenters are often doing silent work, only to be recognized later. "The influence of minorities is indirect, delayed, and not always visible—when these group members are influential, change is often not attributed to their influence," write Jetten and Hornsey. "The value of opinion minorities lies in their ability to guard the group against complacency, to challenge conventional wisdom, and to keep the group sharp and on its toes. In that way, dissenting minorities can change norms or behavioral conventions that have lost their utility."

Another term for a dissenter is a *moral rebel*, defined as "someone who stands up and takes a conspicuous stance in opposition to a norm, expectation, or convention that they perceive to be immoral." A moral rebel can also be called a *positive deviant.* In fact, Stanford professor Benoît Monin and colleagues point out that moral rebellion poses distinct threats to groups, and so dissenters are not always welcome, but they should be. Sometimes, their rebellion is seen as criticism of the group, or their actions make people in the group question their assumptions, or the rebels confront the group in their own complicity with immoral acts, all of which can lead to existential crises, resentment, and defensiveness. "Dissenting minorities exert influence on the group as a whole because they force the majority to think outside the box," write Jetten and Hornsey.

There is certainly an incentive for welcoming dissenters, however. "By tolerating a deviant or dissenter, group members can show that they act in accordance with their beliefs and values, and this strengthens the social fabric of the group," they write. Perhaps we can start to think of dissenters as cheerleaders for humanity?

A concept relatively unheard of now, Jetten and Hornsey also argue that "mindful of the benefits of dissent, some groups might create informal roles within their ranks that free people up to engage in dissent." I haven't seen much of this as an adult, though I recall schoolteachers encouraging dissent during classroom discussions. "An example is the role of court jesters in the Middle Ages who, perhaps because of their marginal and nonthreatening position, were the only ones who were licensed to openly raise unpleasant truths in the presence of the king or queen," they write. "A modern equivalent is the role of the devil's advocate, whose purpose is to question the group's functioning in order to understand the organization's weaknesses."

This raises important questions: Can universities, workplaces, and social media platforms carve out space for dissent? Have we forgotten the value of dissent because we are all so afraid of offending one another? We need to take seriously what it is that we are losing in the face of the crippling fear of being wrong or hurting someone's feelings. We need to cheer on the cheerleaders of humanity.

Champions of Dissent

There are countless examples of individuals and new organizations that champion dissenters, celebrate unconventional viewpoints, and dare to voice opinions that are unpopular to say out loud.

Heterodox Academy is an organization that promotes viewpoint diversity on campuses by building alliances of students, faculty, and administrators who are committed to open inquiry and the exchange of diverse ideas. Another organization is the Foundation for Individual Rights and Expression (FIRE), a legal organization that defends the right of free speech, no matter the issue, and they represent clients from all political parties. Braver Angels is a grassroots organization that brings together laypeople across the political spectrum to gather and connect human to human. These are just a few examples; there are countless more across all industries.

Likewise, journalists, influencers, and podcasters are challenging strongly held ideas and inviting in dissent. Podcaster Coleman Hughes has built a following not only as a rapper, but also by inviting diverse political thinkers onto his show, *Conversations with Coleman*; as an emerging public intellectual trained in philosophy, he has a dedicated audience that appreciates his sharp insights and balanced approach. Influencer Mark Groves, who specializes in relationships and connection, has spoken openly about how important disagreement and authenticity are in building real connections and relationships. The speaker Africa Brooke first chronicled her journey to sobriety online, and in that process realized that her wholeness required her to be authentically herself in all ways, not simply in relation to her recovery; as a Black woman, she was tired of being put into a narrow identity box. Journalist Bari Weiss left the *New York Times* to start the *Free Press* in order to give voice to writers across the political spectrum, not just the far left. While some of these individuals may be considered controversial—and of course many readers will disagree with their work or viewpoints—they have each taken bold steps and attempted in their own way to create platforms for more diverse opinions, away from groupthink.

Meghan Daum is a well-known essayist who has also struck out on her own with *The Unspeakable* podcast, in which she has conversations with artists, entertainers, journalists, scientists, scholars, and anyone else who's willing to do the "unspeakable" and question prevailing cultural and moral assumptions. "I became a writer because I wanted to look at what was going on in the world and actually articulate the truth of it in a way that people maybe didn't even realize they felt that way—or they noticed the same things but they were afraid to say them out loud. I just think that's the job of a creative person, and especially writers," Meghan tells me. "When I started writing in the early '90s, if you were going to write essays to point out certain truths and hypocrisies, that was rewarded. And you'd get another assignment—like, 'job well done.' "

Daum has always been interested in the gap between what people thought they were supposed to think or feel, and what they actually thought and felt. Initially her work was widely published, from the *New York Times* to the *LA Times* and the *New Yorker*. Then around 2014, she started noticing that the air in literary circles changed. Her writer friends would say one thing privately but then say otherwise online. She was deeply perplexed. At around the same time, she describes what happens next as being "recategorized"—that is, because she wasn't a die-hard online social justice activist, she was viewed as problematic. She didn't go along with others, and she kept being herself, publicly, as she always had, unlike many writers she knew. And like others, she has faced backlash for being a "white, hetero, cis" commentator on identity-related matters, but onlookers fail to acknowledge the many diverse voices she features and collaborates with.

Now Meghan is building in-person gatherings across the United States for people to come together and say their own quiet parts out loud that they feel scared to talk about with neighbors and friends. People write to her sharing how alone they feel, and that's where the idea for her gatherings came from. So I ask Meghan what her advice is for other aspiring silence breakers. "Speak up in an intellectually honest way. Don't give in to reductive clickbait talking points," she says. The only way to fight extremism is to fight with nuance, she reiterates.

For Meghan and the many other individuals and organizations advocating for greater viewpoint diversity, there is care, investment, and dedication to the beauty and joy of debate—it's not about featuring wild hate speech, as some narrow-minded opponents might suggest. This is an important distinction, and as readers journey toward greater nuance and critical reasoning, time should be taken to read closely what many of these writers are advocating for.

Pushing Us Forward: Dissent Leads to the Search for Information

The United States, from what I've gathered in my conversations with people for this book, is a country that suffers from a shortage of exposure—exposure to diversity of ideas, backgrounds, and thoughts within one's own neighborhood, school, and workplace. Even with all the diversity, equity, and inclusion work nowadays, because it is often forced and surface-level—relying on rote memorization of talking points as opposed to nuanced inquiry—there doesn't seem to be a real, deeply felt awareness of the feelings and inner lives of others from differing demographics.

Connection, empathy, and understanding stem from sitting with another's reality in a slow, patient way, not simply from reading or watching videos. While there is excellent, nuanced work happening in DEI spaces, it sometimes feels a bit detached. A fantastic 2023 debate at MIT featuring Karith Foster and others highlights the nuances of DEI done well—and done badly. Foster is a diversity engagement specialist who speaks widely on moving from "safe spaces" to "brave spaces," championing authentic expression away from the division that she sees dominating the majority of DEI work, especially from her perspective as a Black woman. As a comedian focused on truth-telling, she brings an appreciation for the nuanced inner experiences of people; as such, the name of her DEI consultancy is "Inversity."

Regarding the value of exposure to diversity of ideas, a 1996 paper by two UC Berkeley researchers states that, "Individuals exposed to minority disagreement have been found to utilize more strategies in the service of performance, recall more information, manifest more flexibility in thought, show more originality and detect solutions that otherwise would have gone undetected."

The UC Berkeley researchers were particularly concerned with exposure to minority dissent on political issues and found that minority dissent tends to "stimulate the search for more information," which is a wonderful outcome and a pursuit we should encourage more of. We want people seeking out information and coming to their own conclusions after thinking critically. Their study offered evidence that people with the minority opinion would be "motivated to understand the majority message and, as such, search for information that would shed light on that position." Can exposure to new or opposing ideas help us get curious about each other rather than more angry or hateful toward one another?

More than twenty years later and in the context of social media, that inclination bears out. In a 2018 study, researchers found that "for some individuals social network diversity . . . is an opportunity to engage in enhanced perspective taking."

While exposure to different perspectives has potential to produce the healthy challenging of ideas and a search for new information, it is the algorithms that often stand in the way. As the researchers write, "Diverse news recommendations can foster increased news exposure," which is great if viewers actually see those diverse news recommendations.

With likes and shares as incentives for individuals, and platforms relying on eyeballs scrolling for as long as possible, the incentives for the platforms themselves is to keep reinforcing what people want to hear—that is, seeing the same echo chamber perspectives over and over. In short, profit motivation drives addiction and outrage. Critical thinking is perilous to the growth of social networks that need to keep users as engaged as possible for the greatest monetary reward. Agree, nod, like, read more, and stay on longer. Thankfully, there are certain settings users can turn on that make updates appear chronologically, not according to what the algorithm perceives the user wants to see.

We should also challenge the notion that subgroups and audiences are so distinct to begin with. In a study out of South Korea, Hanyang University's media and communication professor Dongyoung Sohn writes, "If people are exposed to attitudinally incongruent media . . . they might think that there are fewer people with congruent opinions outside of their local network, causing them to underestimate its proportion in the opinion climate." This is also referred to as pluralistic ignorance, meaning that "people tend to wrongly believe that the majority disapproves of their private opinions when the majority actually supports them. . . . In other words, being exposed to attitudinally incongruent media might cause individuals to underestimate the proportion of congruent people in the general population, lowering their likelihood of speaking out even when they are a local majority."

Sohn created a simulation model to theorize how information spreads across mass media and more local social networks as he wanted to assess how self-silencing ebbs and flows according to prevailing opinion climates. Regarding political and viewpoint diversity, he and his colleagues assert that a slight deviation or introduction to an alternative voice has the power to interrupt the cycle of silence. If there is a dominant narrative in place in a community, a cycle of silence tends to remain entrenched for those with a minority viewpoint; the same is true for those with very close social ties, like we learned with close-knit religious circles—that is, patterns of self-silencing remain because people are afraid to dissent. But what Sohn suggests, however, is that *exposure to alternative viewpoints begins to dissipate the cycle of silence for audiences.* I imagine it like a drop of food coloring in a cup of water; a tiny drop is introduced, swirls around, and changes the color composition completely.

Exposure to diversity of thought in the online world can generally result in one of two directions: a sense of overwhelm or a sense of curiosity and celebration. In the field of online psychology or what is called "cyberpsychology," *context collapse* is a fancy way of referring to when "worlds collide" and can be as simple as the stressful blending of several audiences whereby an individual is forced to manage multiple groups that are normally separate—having family, friends, and coworkers on Facebook is a clear example. On the other hand, researchers Jenny Davis and Nathan Jurgenson coined the term *context collusion* to convey the *strengths* of when all of one's various audiences and networks come together. Bringing together different networks from various contexts can often be enjoyable, and they explain that context collusion has always existed—a wedding, for example, is an *intentional* invitation to many networks to *join together*, which offers a similar comparison for how to think about social media.

Indeed, many people viewed the arrival of social media as a grand virtual party bringing together friends and family across the globe with new ideas, photos, and experiences. Perhaps it's time we embrace that mindset again and learn to metabolize the inevitable awkward or uncomfortable moments that arise. Early online culture felt like a place where people were truly grateful and excited to share simple pleasures—and that ethic, ironically, felt like the ultimate safe space, a space to share joy and curiosity.

But the degradation of online culture, where algorithms thrive on outrage that often tips over into abuse, has meant that some groups of people have had to silo in order to protect themselves. While absolutely necessary at times, this, too, has often resulted in more segregation, not less. That is, absent ill will and ill intent, sharing intense disagreements is different from hate speech, and such sharing can ultimately allow people to better understand one another and overcome tension. So the modern concept of a "safe space," away from *all* potential negativity, is somewhat of a setback for online culture and diversity of thought and discourse. In a 2021 study by Qinfeng Zhu and Marko Skoric, they examine this concept of "safe space" and how political disagreement online drives the creation of such spaces. "Opinion minorities are more inclined to cut ties in the face of political disagreement than the majorities," they write. "People can actively customize their newsfeeds by pruning their online social networks and making ad hoc decisions about who to mute or disconnect from."

It is this pruning of diversity of thought that is dangerous. As they write, "Generally speaking, greater choice often requires stronger filtering capacity, which could potentially lead to an actual reduction in diversity. Since exposure to different views is crucial for cultivating an informed and tolerant citizenry, it is important to understand whether and how social media may promote the creation of homogenous political environments." They argue that "unfriending" people online is a form of selective avoidance—that is, consciously filtering out input that one does not agree with drives a person to retreat into a kind of avoidant state, a "safe space." Their research focused on whether and how often people with "weak ties" would unfriend when encountering political views they disagreed with. They indeed found that weak ties are "particularly weak in the face of political disagreement." Cutting weak ties means less exposure to political diversity. "While selective avoidance may provide an important psychological and social mechanism to defend minority views under certain circumstances, it also prevents people from hearing the other side, which consequently could reinforce existing cleavages and lead to political gridlocks," they write. Exposure is vital for the development of the kind of critical thinking required to communicate with everyone we engage with, and we should carve out spaces for exposure to difference in whatever spheres possible, from our online groups and networks to schools and workplaces, neighborhoods, family gatherings, and more. To be an intellectually honest critical thinker requires the constant discipline of exposure to difference and continually refining the muscle of viewpoint tolerance and engagement with disagreement. Disagreement and conflict can be points of connection and richer understanding.

A paper by psychologist Bert Hodges at University of Connecticut explores the tension between conformity and dissent; Hodges argues that both are present and are woven into social relations all the time, as opposed to what traditional theories have said—that people fall into one camp or another: conformists or dissenters. "Divergence is as pervasive as convergence," he states. That is, we can all be followers *and* leaders. You might more often dissent when a topic tugs at a cause you care about but choose to conform when the stakes are lower, for example. "Social understanding cannot be reduced to convergence or divergence." There is an embeddedness and an interdependency involved in all interactions and forms of thought such that we are in constant dialogue, feeding off one another—and this becomes a different way to view critical thought and free speech. Dissenting is not equivalent to being a loner or outcast; it is a stake in the ground from which others can view, reflect, argue, debate, and ultimately learn much more about the world, themselves, and other people. By building the muscle of tolerance through exposure to disagreement and difference, our joyful party of dissenters gets stronger, louder, and freer.

Chapter 5

The Courage to Stand Alone

Many people today find themselves feeling uneasy, not only in the face of nonstop global news and information streaming toward them from their phones, as social science research shows, but our hyper-connected modern era can also make us feel as though there is a general sense of tension and malaise in the air. It's almost as though our internal skeletal structures lack the solidity to face the scale of information presented before us, and indeed research from psychologist and Yeshiva University professor Sabrina Romanoff indicates that overwhelm can lead to a state of shutdown, paralysis, and fatigue.

In contrast, I think of large animal skeletons hanging inside natural history museums, where you can imagine the strength to bend and charge that dinosaurs, sharks, and woolly mammoths all possess. For lack of a better description, nowadays, many of us humans seem to be missing an emotional backbone, made worse by the onslaught of unfiltered information.

It is not easy to question established doctrine, to apply critical reasoning to the kaleidoscope of information around us. Entertaining critical thought on an ongoing basis can be lonely, isolating, confusing, and disorienting. Fortifying an emotional backbone is thus central to building critical thinking habits (and critical speaking habits), and it's helpful to better understand the necessary components of autonomy and individuation as one sets out to build these muscles. It's also important to understand what human beings are up against, psychologically, when attempting to overcome self-silencing.

It's possible that people who have been particularly enmeshed within groupthink have more of a hurdle to overcome right off the bat. In my encounters with "group exiters," both in interviews and in reading studies on them, it felt clear to me that some aspect of development seemed temporarily hindered, as though a blockage was present due to the impact of long-term subscription to a well-defined thought framework. It was virtually impossible for some people to think for themselves for a period of time. A helplessness was present, as though the muscle of critical reasoning hadn't been exercised and so attempts at thinking on one's own felt scary and frightening, like stepping foot into a body of water for the first time, never having played or swam in a river or pool before. While research on this area is scarce, lawyers and other individuals who handle international extremist cases are aware of the impact that extremist ideology has on parenting, for example. A 2024 *Family & Law* article by researchers in the Netherlands indicates that the successful transfer of violent ideology to children is a known risk but because the long-term impact is difficult to quantify, legal policies about how to intervene have not been agreed upon.

Groupthink, in many ways, does not allow you to develop your own skin. It is thus a form of injury; it leaves a wound as it disables your ability to think for yourself. Additionally, ideological myopia itself is a form of dissociation: It sweeps the mind away from the body, preventing the detection and feeling of what is occurring within oneself in the present moment.

Psychologist Marlene Winell is a leading religious trauma psychologist and workshop facilitator for people who have left behind fundamentalism and Evangelicalism, herself having been raised abroad by missionaries. In one of her videos, she refers to this same sense of "developmental delay" that happens for exiters because they have been cocooned for so long. An audience member pipes up, saying it feels like having "training wheels" on all the time when protected by religion. There is a real "coming down to earth" process, away from magical thinking, that forces people to encounter the messier sides of life. People can feel like small children again.

The coming down to earth part is almost literal: staring at trees, marveling at animals, recognizing one's own animal nature. It's sobering. In many ways, this is the exact process we might experience if we detox from the groupthink of social media or our political bubbles, family belief systems, unhealthy friend groups or coworkers, or any setting in which group ideologies take hold. I have found in my own life that returning to daily walks, traveling, spending time with animals, and enjoying quiet time help keep me in tune with my own body, and with reality. Winell actually verbalizes this as well in her videos, saying, "Be a good animal." Every single individual at some point realizes they are an animal. We all have this in common. It is unifying and powerful. We are beings navigating land and terrain and complex ecosystems and interpersonal dynamics.

"Individuation" itself can be thought of as growing from childhood to adolescence to adulthood, from college to work life, or from being intensely ideological to becoming more of a critical thinker. The goal is to get comfortable with standing in one's own self, thought process, and even sense of physical presence. In some ways, the process of breaking through self-silencing is about getting grounded, truly planted in the here and now, away from whatever swirls of culture surround you.

It is scary and daunting to step out into the unknown, and to develop the intellectual agility to pivot and lean into uncertainty; I think of a dancing figure bending their body forward, backward, and side to side as streams of ideas come at them, and they develop their own rhythm as they adapt to the torrent. It is exceedingly rewarding to engage in the dance, and to feel such a strong backbone form. Another way to think about this is a dancer lighting up the steps beneath their feet with sound in an array of colors—the more they dance, the more they learn what melody resonates and what they truly think and believe.

It's important to not skip over this step and jump from escaping groupthink to spouting loud dissenting opinions prematurely. There is a crucial in-between process that is internal; it is about developing critical thinking skills so your individual opinions are fully formed. Only then can you take seriously your own observations and real-world experiences and thus develop the confidence and intellectual flexibility to move through the world with your critical thinking intact. In other words, people need to feel a sense of safety in letting their thoughts wander and arrive at their own conclusions and then, hopefully, they can share them with others or build work and hobbies around such freethinking. Sharing ideals of debate and critical thinking with others can be a first step toward inviting more honesty and authenticity into friendships, workplace dynamics, and family settings. By creating the space for self-silencing to fade, people gain practice in taking off their masks. And when first starting out, people will fumble by coming across harshly or swinging to the other extreme from their former viewpoint as they learn to question, but the more people practice, the more they find their own center.

Remember when doing this work: Questions matter. Doubts matter. Arrive at your own conclusions. A person doesn't have to blindly buy into the viewpoints from any side that dominates, whether regarding abortion, trans issues, race, gender, education, guns, or the environment. Issues are not just political—they are human—and it's vital to drill down into one's own heart and mind, and fully unpack these questions for yourself. Just like the many deconverters out there, everyone should feel permitted to push back, shed outdated frameworks, and speak up accordingly. At the end of one's journey into critical thought, a person may find that they do indeed agree with most of the framework they grew up with or what their community believes. Or they may find that their critical reasoning leads them to significantly diverge. It can be frightening to entertain your doubts, but ultimately you'll be a healthier person. Stick with complexity, and stay curious.

Developing Autonomy

Social scientists study a known phenomenon called *mortality salience*, which refers to how aware and sensitive an individual is to their own mortality (i.e., their eventual demise and the inevitability of death). That got me thinking about something I'll call *aliveness salience* (i.e., being awake to one's own life and individuality).

Many who struggle with self-silencing do not fully embrace reality; their aliveness salience is low. And I mean the basic tenets of reality: we are born, we struggle, we die. Pleasure, joy, and meaning exist along the way, but death is real, failure is real, accidents happen, and the endurance of all these things is vital, inescapable. Self-censorship is a way of resisting reality, keeping distanced from the here and now that might stare a person in the face and force them to confront their innermost thoughts and feelings. That said, when one is finally able to embrace reality, whether by encountering pain or through some kind of close encounter with death or overcoming severe hardship, the individual becomes emboldened, less fearful, and able to face reality with greater strength.

And then comes the journey to autonomy.

Autonomy, I believe, is a natural developmental inclination, just as natural as the drive to belong. They may seem like opposing desires, but in fact, among the many theorists discussing the concept of autonomy today, many agree that with autonomy comes the belief that *humans are also deeply interdependent*. We want to be individuals but not isolated. So we have a perfect, organic setup for the antithesis of self-silencing; that is, that one must find out who they are and voice who they are, while still remaining in close ties with other human beings *regardless of whether they share common views or not*. This is beautiful, and perfect: to exist as you, and still find love and kinship and friendship, respect and belonging, despite disagreement.

According to leading autonomy researcher Professor Richard M. Ryan of the University of Rochester and his colleagues, "When persons act autonomously, they feel 'wholehearted,' 'together,' and 'ownership of their actions,' all common expressions that convey the characteristic sense of integrity and volition essential to autonomy." As one of the developers of self-determination theory (SDT), Ryan's research has been central to understanding intrinsic motivation, self-determination, and autonomy. He and his colleagues report that when acting autonomously, people function fully in alignment, "undivided" as they pursue their goals. I take their exploration and definition of autonomy to capture what it feels like once a person can transcend self-silencing. For example, they write, "Autonomy is a quality of regulation, characterized by an open processing of possibilities and a matching of these with sensibilities, needs, and known constraints."

Ryan developed SDT along with his colleague Edward Deci after he had initially studied philosophy and then later worked with people with developmental disabilities. The going theory of motivation at the time, in the 1970s, was that people were driven by rewards—in other words, reinforcement behavior, external incentives like grades, money, attractiveness, status, hierarchy, and similar factors. But Ryan and Deci wanted to bring attention to internal factors that seemed inherent in many people they worked with—things like creativity, drive, and other intrinsic motivators. Thus, the intrinsic/extrinsic framework was born and SDT was developed as a larger umbrella for research and practice.

SDT is now a successful approach within research and psychology, and the pair of researchers have been cited thousands of times over the decades. There are conferences and workshops, extensive trainings, and international talks. According to their website, SDT "begins with the assumption that people are active organisms, with evolved tendencies toward growing, mastering ambient challenges, and integrating new experiences into a coherent sense of self. These natural developmental tendencies do not, however, operate automatically, but instead require ongoing social nutriments and supports." This approach and philosophy sounds surprisingly similar to the conclusions I had been coming to myself after observing modern trends of mental health, well-being, and self-silencing. According to SDT, healthy development rests on autonomy, competence, and relatedness—that is, a healthy sense of individuality, a confidence in knowing how to accomplish things in life, and an ability to connect with others. The less these are developed, the more problems people will face, and the more these traits are developed, the more success they will find in life. I would argue that all three of these traits contribute to having a strong emotional backbone.

Interestingly, autonomy is deeply challenging for some people with neurodevelopmental differences. In *Divergent Mind,* I spend considerable time examining interdependence, the need for greater understanding about different processing speeds, acceptance of oneself, and accepting logistical help from others when needed. What helps all people gain greater autonomy, especially neurodivergent people, is for one's genuine inner motivators and passions to find authentic expression—that is, for the quiet, hidden, somewhat "niche" interests to emerge fully either in work or hobbies. Too many people—especially neurodivergent folks who are taught to mask or hide their "special interests"—are silencing an inborn aspect of themselves that would otherwise likely result in a healthier outcome if expressed. There are ways in which one's obsessive focus can result in work and career and in that way lead to autonomy. In my own life, as I discuss in *Divergent*

Mind, having fulfilling work has been crucial for the autonomy it provides, both existentially and practically.

It turns out that tuning in to one's own intrinsic motivation is a key aspect of autonomy. Whatever your obsession is, what is it about it that drives you? If fashion, is it the feel of the materials or the way people look at you in your outfit? If birdwatching, is it the diversity of feathers, the feel of the wind, or the peaceful silence of the hills and trees? As I shared in *Divergent Mind*, curiosity about the inner lives of others has always been a main driver for me. The intrinsic motivation to want to know more has ultimately led to a career in writing and interviewing. Not only is my curiosity satisfied, but I also earn a living at it in many creative forms, from writing books to lecturing and speaking.

Finding one's path, especially with the financial component intact, gives a person a feeling of confidence, empowerment, autonomy, and what some might call "self-actualization." And it is key to not hide away from whatever your "thing" is. Keep at it. As Ryan et al. write, "These innate or natural tendencies are intrinsically motivated in the sense that they require no incentives or pressures but instead occur spontaneously when the social context does not forestall them."

However, when the natural inclinations of individuals that would otherwise lead to greater autonomy are instead thwarted in some way, bad things happen. "Intrinsic motivation—and the curiosity, assimilative tendency, and joy that attend it—have been predicted to be undermined in conditions that are overly controlling or inconsistent, leading to nonoptimal development and, in extreme cases, the onset of stagnation and psychopathology." This is once again key for our discussion of self-silencing, because many people are swimming in such a climate. I would argue that social media is largely about being controlled, even when people think they are openly expressing themselves. In a climate of self-silencing, where people know what is acceptable to say or not, people inadvertently censor out of fear of being canceled, mobbed, or ostracized. Such a culture is the antithesis of the kinds of conditions needed to nurture autonomy.

No Person Is an Island

Much of the "reward" for staying silent about one's true beliefs is membership in the tribe, but that is not real belonging and there are alternative ways to be oneself and stay connected to others. Learning to overcome self-silencing while at the same time still being mindful of others and participating in active social life and community is a dance, and it's more easily accomplished when one has a solid sense of autonomy amid social connectedness. The feeling of connection is not based on sharing the same views or agreeing on everything. How many family members do you love with all your heart and yet vehemently disagree with about politics? For many families, this is a widely understood feature of family life, and many are able to joke about it, leading to funny holiday stories, opinion pieces in local newspapers, and memes. Engaging in such dynamics leads to more self-certainty because the muscle of viewpoint tolerance is being flexed and one's own backbone and sense of self-agency and confidence are able to stay intact. Remaining connected to others across differences is a vital exercise that enriches us as individuals and as communities. In fact, holding viewpoint diversity as a family value can go a long way in encouraging healthy autonomy, because both connectedness *and* individuality are simultaneously supported.

At the core of developing autonomy is also the process of internalization—that is, integrating what one learns from the environment about how to succeed, and then integrating one's unique way of being into those processes. In workplaces, if someone is new to office life, they may have concerns about office hierarchy, but over time they may come to appreciate the order and consistency it offers. When one is resistant from the get-go, it is more difficult to function, get along, learn from bosses and mentors, keep the job, and develop autonomy while integrating into the new setting. This is not the same as someone becoming a robot, but it is the process of negotiating what is necessary in order to get along with others in society while at the same time being their own person, with their own individual personality and way of doing things and getting things done.

Psychologist Valerie Tarico also emphasizes that part of individuation is learning to live with uncertainty and complexity and the way that real life defies categories and simple answers. "Simple answers to complicated problems can be worse than no answers at all. To steer the direction of our lives we have to understand the complex causality that governs our well-being. That includes factors that are in our own control as well as those that are not," she writes.

An attitude of radical acceptance can also aid autonomy. It may be helpful to look at shedding inherited identities and beliefs as part of the natural life cycle. A person can choose to keep traditions, but part of the gift of modern adult life is not feeling beholden to do so. For example, people who are gay and grow up in less-accepting towns might now feel at liberty to choose to live life in a community that is open and accepting of their sexuality, allowing them to live life openly gay. Likewise, a person of Jewish descent can choose atheism but still stay close to their family in other ways. As Tarico writes, "Individuation means forming a self that gets to choose which of these old messages, beliefs and habit patterns to carry forward. It means discovering that I am not my parents or other ancestors (or my peer group). Their hopes, beliefs, habits, sins, traumas, wounds, and coping mechanisms don't have to be mine. I do not even have to be my old self if I don't want to."

On Individuation

Becoming an individual can be a scary, daunting experience for some, especially when raised or immersed in environments where groupthink was deeply entrenched. Imagine a theoretical ocean creature emerging onto land for the first time with new legs, or a baby emerging into fresh air after the all-encompassing cradle of the womb. The sensations that accompany becoming your own person as an adult, in the face of challenging conversations with friends or family, can be overwhelming. How do you manage boundaries or feelings of confusion, or perhaps even anger from someone you are speaking with?

There are different ways to think about individuation; imagining yourself as a rooted tree can be helpful, standing upright with your trunk strong. And perhaps at the next family gathering a group comes up to you and makes the case for why everyone should go to church for Christmas, even though it's the only day of the year that your family does this, and no one thinks much about their Christian identity beyond that one day. Perhaps you are at a point where you feel like attending on Christmas isn't really bringing the family closer together or serving your emotional or spiritual needs and you've already decided you don't want to attend. If there are four people in front of you, and you are the only one dissenting, what do you do? What do you say?

At this point, in order to deepen the conversation to take everyone to a new level of thinking about the tradition, you can use your own insight into your interior, emotional experience to help you communicate and share your experience and reflections, which usually paves the way for others to open up in a more thoughtful way—and everyone now gets to be individuals at the table. What this looks like is taking a breath, centering yourself, letting your mental awareness sink into your heart—literally imagining your chest and the center of your body—and then sharing your thoughts and feelings from that place. Perhaps it might sound like, "I really treasure you all. I miss you, and we don't get to spend enough time together. I know attending church has been our tradition in the past. But I'm wondering how we all feel now that we're older and what everyone's thoughts are on making the most of our time together." This is a truthful, vulnerable way to communicate that is authentic and allows for others to respond from the heart and from their individual viewpoint. And because you have set the tone in a heart-centered way, others then feel safe and like they have the chance to respond with new thoughts and ideas. By leading with heart and employing critical thinking, we start to change the norms and culture around us.

An essential part of the process of individuation is trusting yourself, staying true to yourself, and being able to communicate your truth. It may take time for others to develop the skill of holding complexity and balancing heartfelt communication with critical reasoning, but gradually, over time, everyone gains exposure in how to be an individual—and a more genuine connection is built with others.

Resisting Contorting Ourselves Online

We can also take steps toward staying true to our individuality online in the face of massive social media pressure to contort ourselves. From a social science perspective, there are terms used in the cyberpsychology literature that are instrumental in helping us to understand how exactly we shape-shift under the pressure of the online world. *Impression management*, for example, refers to the management of how one is perceived by others online, which relates to *self-presentation*, or how one presents oneself.

From a research perspective, the issue of self-presentation online poses challenges. If we are all wearing metaphorical masks, how does anyone get at the truth? Researchers Margeret Hall and Simon Caton wrote in 2017 that "the trove of potential online social media data is vast, but the ability of researchers identifying ground truth models, and thus to verify its authenticity, is low."

According to Bangkok-based philosophy professor Soraj Hongladarom, "The emergence of social networking sites has created a problem of how the self is to be understood in the online world. . . . There seems to emerge a new kind of self which exists in the online world. . . . The line between the two kinds of self is becoming fuzzier. Furthermore, there seems to be a fusion between the online and the offline selves, which reflects the view that reality itself is informational." A Thai philosopher, Hongladarom states that many in Thailand create entirely new personas that exist exclusively online, largely because free speech laws are so restrictive. Active social media users there have thus become extremely "creative," in his words. Deeply concerned with the exact nature and definition of the "self," he writes, "The online self is a kind of persona that an individual makes up as a front to present himself or herself to the world, and sometimes the individual may intend it that the persona assume an identity of its own, without being able to refer back to the real person behind."

In a discussion of online identity reconstruction in *Frontiers in Psychology*, Jiao Huang et al. write that "individuals who are not satisfied with certain characteristics of themselves are more likely to engage in self-enhancement online." This is particularly relevant for adolescents, who use the internet to explore their own identity more than other age groups.

A 2020 paper from University of Wolverhampton psychology professor Chris Fullwood and colleagues across the US and Australia suggests that "individuals with higher self-concept clarity and self-monitoring are more likely to present a single consistent online and offline self. Younger adults and those with greater social anxiety are more likely to present idealized self-images online, and participants with higher social anxiety and lower self-esteem are more likely to prefer online, rather than offline, communication." They cite research on impression management, saying that "the 'actor' will wear the 'mask' most appropriate to the communication context they find themselves in." Additionally, they state that "presenting idealized self-images may be the default self-presentation position when one is unclear on how to present the self to others, which could explain why younger individuals with a less clear sense of self are more prone to engage in this behavior."

There is both a positive side and negative side to identity experimentation online. They write, "Adults who possess a less clear sense of who they are may benefit, in the same way as adolescents have been shown to, from taking opportunities to try out different self-presentations online as an act of self-discovery. Having lower self-esteem, however, may also suggest that some of these individuals are catering their self-presentation styles to different audiences in a bid for approval, perhaps because they are doubtful of being able to make the types of impressions they desire to make."

This is all depressing, of course, because catering self-presentation to audiences just means more performing, less authenticity, and a less stable emotional backbone. That said, if the experimentation is temporary, perhaps it's less worrisome? Are people experiencing delayed identity experimentations online that they weren't able to try out in real life when younger? I can see the positives and negatives. Certainly, some of it seems natural and healthy; where I'm worried is when it becomes excessive.

Additionally, if identity tends to be temporary, and yet we immortalize ourselves through our digital footprints, posting things on social media and updating our LinkedIn profiles, it can be difficult to feel the temporary nature of identity stages—and it can also feel tricky to know how to "refashion" ourselves online given the digital time stamps of our various identity phases. Should we all go back and delete or rewrite ourselves?

Researchers in Europe conducted a study in which they took a small sample of journalists from Norway and Spain who had been working in the media for between six months and three years, chosen because of their experience having to manage their online reputations as newly public figures and also because of their recent transitions from university student to professional. Interestingly, their identity experimentations were indeed temporary. "The participants expressed clear concern about how digital traces from their youth were incompatible with their current brand and reputation as professional journalists and, as such, complicated their self-presentation. . . . Most of our study participants reported concerns about future negative reactions to old content and expressions from their youthful experimentations. Some noted they had shared risky content in the past, while others simply found their past content to be embarrassing." They continue, "Our participants described their experiences of this muddling of time through their concerns about negative reactions to old content. In other words, this concern was about how playful or experimenting self-expression from the past could hurt their future professional identity or their identity in general."

Unsurprisingly, and while this was not the focus of the study, the participants were all concerned about being "canceled." "What's on my Instagram, I don't really care about, but Twitter makes me paranoid," one writer shared. They also discuss a feeling of needing to "keep the peace" as they post and share online, which researchers conclude can affect both mental health and actual participation in society and politics, given such feelings of strain and restraint. Importantly, they conclude, "our participants described how they curated their image and self-censored both their previous and current self-generated content. Interestingly, some reported feeling trapped by their own online identity in social media."

In other cases, over in Australia and the US, Fullwood et al. found that "individuals with a more stable sense of self may convey images that are congruent with their own self-perceptions online and offline, because they are confident about who they are and expect to be accepted by others."

But many people do indeed resort to censoring themselves in real time in accordance with whatever platform and audience they are encountering in an effort to manage and control. In a joint paper, a group of researchers at the University of Edinburgh and the University of Birmingham in the UK refer to self-censorship as avoidance-based self-regulation (ABSR)—that is, tailoring, curating, and editing one's presence online as a strategy of audience and impression management. "In order to maintain a desired image, users act (or refrain from acting) to avoid projecting one which is undesired," they write. However, worryingly, they write that "widespread adoption of ABSR may result in a 'lowest common denominator' effect, where users tend to project the 'safest' self-presentation to meet the expectations of their strictest audience." This captures the plague of self-silencing. If we're constantly monitoring, changing, and shape-shifting, how can we ever authentically share ourselves, or know whether others are being truthful about who they are?

The researchers also examine a process known as *self-focused attention (SFA)* which is thought to be the mechanism whereby a social media user would eventually censor themselves online. SFA refers to the awareness on the individual's part of not only her own internal feelings but also those of her audience, in this case doing quick calculations on everyone from her mother to her boss and boyfriend, and then posting carefully accordingly. Their study only involved forty university students in England, but in keeping with other research findings, their worry is that "peer-to-peer surveillance has the potential to be oppressive and anxiety provoking." Again, if no one is being honest, we're all walking around on eggshells about what's real, and that doesn't make anyone feel safe. We are all nervous wrecks as a result.

They continue, "Offline and online lives are becoming increasingly blurred, with the growing prevalence of mobile technologies and drive to make content instantly communicable online through links with online personas. Given this, public SFA may begin to increase in wider circumstances. . . . A recent account in the media suggests that offline avoidance-based regulation may already be taking place because of the saliency of online audiences." That is, people are altering their offline behavior because of increasingly controlling and prevalent social norms online, which is a frightening development. It's as though humanity is now allowing the algorithms to dictate culture itself.

The researchers' particular tips to combat the blurring of realities and the resulting self-censorship are to set privacy settings to be able to post to one's different audiences (for impression management and to prevent context collapse), select tag settings such that your tagged photos from one audience are not shown to an undesired audience, and adopt a "think twice, post once" policy so that one can better manage impressions as a way to reach who you want to reach and more authentically connect with that particular set of people in your life. These are ways to be more intentional and authentic in communicating with very different parts of one's community. It's not that one hides behind such tools; it's merely avoiding confusion, since naturally the kind of content shared with a parent might be very different from sharing with a partner, colleague, or friend. Leveraging the audience-sharing tools in fact makes one's online experience more reflective of real, offline interactions, since a conversation or story shared with, say, a parent at home, will be different from one shared with a friend at a party. Next time you log onto one of your social media accounts, take a closer look at your settings before you post, select which audience makes sense (Is this public? Or only for a few close friends?), and then "think twice" about what you're posting.

All that said, in our journey to develop a backbone and think and speak more genuinely, there is hope. Many individuals, organizations, writers, journalists, and advocates are leading the way in their walk toward empowered autonomy over the shell of silencing.

Speaking for Yourself

I stumbled upon an article from Japan-based writer David McElhinney after a 2023 eruption over pop singer Gwen Stefani's comments about feeling like she was part Japanese due to her adoration and absorption of the culture since her father often traveled there for business and she grew up integrating Japanese aesthetics into her shows. Publishing in *Al Jazeera*, McElhinney's straightforward article interviewing Japanese people in Japan, where they expressed joy about Stefani's love for their culture, intrigued me. His was a balanced, reasonable article not arguing for whether she was culturally appropriating or not, but rather doing what journalists are supposed to do: getting different perspectives and putting them down on the page. "In Japan, the controversy has barely registered a blip," he wrote in the piece. "Japanese media have largely ignored the Stefani interview, with the only references to the controversy appearing on small webzines and blogs." McElhinney describes the term *cultural appropriation* as a "once-obscure academic term that has moved from US university departments into the Western mainstream," and one of his interviewees shares that "most Japanese are neither familiar with nor sensitive about cultural appropriation."

I decided to get on the phone with McElhinney from his Tokyo home. He tells me, "I don't really think too much about it before I write something like this. We live in a world where no matter what you write, people are going to get upset." He's quick to clarify that this is not an opinion piece. It's reporting on what local Japanese people thought about Gwen Stefani's comments—"And people still got pissed."

"I inoculate myself by not really being on social media," he says. And it's true—he's virtually nonexistent on social media, a rarity for journalists these days. It's only when he met up with a couple of journalist buddies in Tokyo that they mentioned the article's somewhat controversial nature to him. "Did people get annoyed?" he had to ask them. His disconnect from social media is refreshing.

But, he says, the fact that people were getting annoyed proves the point of his article: The people who were annoyed were Western expats in Japan, not local Japanese. "It's largely a Western preoccupation," he emphasizes.

"The word *controversial* is an interesting one. What exactly was I contravening? We're looking at what a particular woman has said about her desire or feeling that she is kind of Japanese. People are saying, 'You can't say that,' but the Japanese are saying, 'Actually we don't really mind.' So, to me, the controversial point is people telling Japanese what they ought to think about someone so-called appropriating their own culture. To me that's more controversial," he says, eloquently. "The word gets thrown around these days, but I think it's lost all meaning," he adds.

And he's sympathetic to people feeling like they're walking around on eggshells, especially in the United States, but what he doesn't understand is how a society that fought for centuries for individual freedom and liberal democracy now prioritizes group identity, group affiliation, and groupthink. "It's so unfree and bizarre," he reiterates.

Conversely, McElhinney is comfortable going against the grain. "My family are all actors, so I grew up in very liberal circles. In my generation, growing up in Northern Ireland, there wasn't huge pressure on the line of work to choose," he begins.

"When you grow up with parents who are actors, it was middle class, and certainly unconventional in a lot of ways. I think I've always been somewhat anti-authority. I don't like being told what to say or what to think. So that sensibility naturally dovetails with the idea that, if I write something, I want to write what I believe and what my thoughts are at the time," he says. And he adds that sometimes his ideas change, but he accepts that as part of nuanced inquiry and discourse. "I think if your identity is based on the group rather than a more individualistic way of looking at things, then you probably struggle to ever look back and say you got it wrong, because the group perhaps doesn't necessarily facilitate that." And, he adds, "if you're willing to censor yourself, then you certainly open yourself up to the idea of letting yourself be censored by others."

While some might argue that the debate over cultural appropriation—that is, that some think it's not acceptable to utilize components of another culture for one's own purposes—warrants larger discussion, McElhinney raises a core point about who exactly is concerned about such interference. If white American expats in Japan are upset over a white woman's comments about her affinity for Japanese culture, but the very people they're trying to supposedly "protect"—Japanese people—do not mind, then isn't their concern more of a puritan form of *saviorism* as opposed to a stance of diplomatic support?

This is yet another example where rigidity of thought resembles religiosity, and the failure to challenge such ingrained concepts limits our ability to connect and objectively assess reality. The courage to stand alone rests on the ability to tolerate disapproval while holding firm in one's values.

Chapter 6

Staying True to Ourselves

As we reflect on our public and private lives, the role of technology, the intimidating noise of groupthink, and hopeful characters who may help us wander through—from journalists to therapists—it's important to take a moment to reflect on what we've learned about dissent and autonomy, the pushback we might feel on a daily basis, and what we might be able to do *to stay true to ourselves.* While we can acknowledge the potential power of connection that the online world has brought about, it's important to be sober about the dark side of the internet and learn how to better ride the many waves of psychological pressures that the internet brings forth.

Brené Brown, for example, through her viral TED talks and now bestselling books, catalyzed a culture change making it safer to be authentic in multiple spheres of life. But as with other culture changes—and the platforms that made them possible, like Facebook, for example, that started out with inspiring intentions to connect the world—Brown's revolution of vulnerability has tipped over into harder territory, because in the hands of an outraged public, the definition and use of *vulnerability* has drastically changed. For some, being "vulnerable" now means oversharing to capture algorithms and attention. What started out as an exercise in expressing genuine sadness or frustration has now, for some internet users, tipped over into distortion and overexaggeration. That is, whereas being "open" about one's mental health status was highly taboo and frowned upon until the explosion of social media in the 2010s, social media is now leveraged to gain clicks and likes through constant sharing of intense emotion, leading to a kind of weaponization of vulnerability, as opposed to it being a vehicle for genuine healing and connection. If a person is rude at work and gets in trouble but that person then goes online claiming to be a victim and falsely claims they have depression, they will get an entirely different response than if they take responsibility and ask for feedback about how to improve their rude behavior. In the case of the former, with an exaggerated claim of depression, support and solidarity often ensue out of sympathy, but with the latter—a request for feedback—there is an opportunity for real, tangible behavioral and life change that helps the individual learn how to handle themselves. But if we're not true to ourselves to begin with, no one on social media can provide the actual support we need for personal growth and well-being.

So now, how do we stay true to ourselves in a sea of such influential pressures, from social media content to our very real urges for connection and belonging? How do we hold on to a more long-term commitment to truth, humility, integrity, and revealing our full, complex selves, as opposed to only a small piece or facade?

Brené Brown herself says, "Vulnerability without boundaries is not vulnerability." And in my view, one of the challenges we are up against in our long-term commitment to the future of human integrity is a problem of "trauma dilution," where distortions and exaggerations make discerning the truth of others' experiences rather difficult as we wade through a sea of shell-like identities at the bottom of the ocean floor. Our task then simultaneously becomes how to break out of those shells and present our deeper selves to the world, but also to learn ways to find others who are also committed to truth, integrity, and authenticity. These are not easy tasks. It's hard to take stock of one's internal world and then communicate from that place. It's much easier to lash out.

It's also easy to lash out in our current climate because there is a whole new class of experts and "influencers" online—from outrage-led activists to poorly informed therapists—whose messaging is steeped in short-term defiance. "Everybody should hate this person who did this bad thing," is a very different message from, "Let's examine the facts of what happened, learn all sides, check in with ourselves about how we feel about the situation, and then let's direct our energy toward the best possible takeaway or resolution for all involved." Because we lack a commitment to the latter nuanced approach, the long-term goals of complex thinking and communicating become more challenging to reach.

Getting Real with Ourselves

Showing intense emotion is often easier than revealing sadness or grief, and it's easier to let the anger and rage take over and show that to the world, letting people think they're seeing "the real you." And it's this intense outrage that may aid in giving rise to cancel culture, because people often cope with sadness and grief in unhealthy ways, channeling their fear and regret into bullying and mobbing. *Social media is one huge dumping ground for everyone's baggage, and yet no one has the tools to deal with their own pain.* Paradoxically, there is a kind of "misalignment" in the timelines and trajectories of the rapidly developed sharing technologies and devices on the one hand, and the abilities of their human users to process emotion and regulate in mature ways on the other. It's all out of sync, users are still catching up, and we need more resources to help people do the vital inner work that can, and should, accompany the sharing that occurs on social media in attempts to connect and heal.

Related to self-regulation, a harmful feature of our technology-powered culture of sharing is how vocabulary is taken from academia and then overemployed or used as scapegoats for those more subtle emotions that are hard to name or contextualize; confusion, overwhelm, sadness, fear, and uncertainty are all much more difficult to name than merely blurting out phrases from research in the mental health field like, "Stop gaslighting me! Stop being such a narcissist!" That is, psychological terminology crosses over from academia to easily accessible social media and makes people feel equipped with the armor of fancy words, but the big words hide deeper feelings of pain, grief, and disregard. Much like conflict between two individuals, the expression of outrage sounds like fights that many couples have, always dodging the harder, vulnerable parts of disagreements.

But the danger is that this is now happening on a mass scale, across the internet. It's no wonder headlines abound regarding the "end of truth" and a "post-truth" era. People literally hold the power to radically redefine reality with the tips of their fingers, including shifting blame at all times and never taking responsibility or interrogating one's inner beliefs and viewpoints.

Therapists are not immune to this way of thinking either as they, too, are on social media, overexposed to terms like *boundaries*, *codependency*, *gaslighting*, and *narcissism*. Of course, there is much value in understanding all of these facets of the human condition, but when people land in therapists' offices, it becomes all too easy to fall into the trap of pointing the finger at actors outside themselves, rather than doing the hard work of confronting ourselves and learning self-agency as a result. And what then happens is a kind of globalizing effect where everything is others' fault. This globalizing effect has never sat well with me—it's reductionist, oversimplified, and reliant on a kind of easy black-and-white thinking that eschews complexity. This kind of "mass blaming" is what is being mirrored on the larger stage. Every upset is someone else's fault. I see this every day on social media where therapists encourage severing ties, eschewing the very connections that help us feel whole, even if those connections are not perfect. Tolerance for difference, uncertainty, and imperfection are vital and yet all too easy to toss to the side nowadays.

A *Chicago Tribune* article by Nick Haslam argues that the "intense focus" on blaming everything on how others have harmed a person has "worrying implications." By blaming others, it's all too easy to conclude that our own issues must be trauma inflicted on us by other people. It's scary because of course trauma should be taken seriously, but if using that word is a way to blame others instead of looking within, then that contributes to the ever-evolving distortion happening across social media and offline. It is very difficult to tell what's real. "Trauma is a way to explain life's problems as someone else's fault," Haslam writes. Likewise, the psychologist Paul Marsden is quoted in a *Metro* article saying that blame culture and the distortion of trauma—that is, exaggerating everyday unpleasant occurrences—"is a real hazard in that it contributes to this kind of pathologisation of life, where we want to give things a label, and the normal stresses and strains of life we want to turn into a pathology by giving it a label. . . . You get a sense of what psychologists call learned helplessness." There is no attempt to excavate what's real anymore, leaving our understanding of ourselves and others empty and barren. People can be afraid to question these trends out loud, because no one wants to appear insensitive. But it is these hard questions that will help us better understand ourselves and each other. Being honest with ourselves and with each other leads to real connection, healing, and belonging. We must learn to be open to being challenged, and that is our best way of knowing ourselves and others. "How did I contribute to this conflict? How did I misinterpret what they said? What is my outrage protecting me from feeling?" These are all questions we must become comfortable asking ourselves on our journeys to greater integrity, empathy, self-management, and tolerance. If we are to overcome self-silencing, we must become better investigators of truth and reality, and that requires developing the skill to look internally and parse through our contributions to our own suffering, what suffering is the result of others' actions, and what negative feelings are simply mundane, unpleasant occurrences that are part of being a human who is navigating life alongside billions of other people. In other words, to overcome self-silencing, we must try our best to get real with ourselves, clear our own lenses, and communicate from that place—not from a place of blame and confusion.

Helpful Reframes

The psychologist Valerie Tarico knows firsthand the impact of groupthink and what it takes to break away. A former Evangelical Christian, she is the author of *Trusting Doubt: A Former Evangelical Looks at Old Beliefs in a New Light*, and she has since explored the wisdom of the great religious teachings from a secular angle. She also writes extensively about how extremist ideology infiltrates the mind, and how this manifests in modern social discourse online and offline.

Tarico is particularly concerned by how excessive categories, cancel culture, self-silencing, and social media all combine to create the same kind of religious self-censorship and intolerance that she has written so extensively about from her own Evangelical community. In her writing and advocacy, she explores the mental health consequences of extreme ideological capture and illustrates the ways that extreme modern movements rely on an emotionally unhealthy architecture that gets reinforced repeatedly online—not only for trolls and mob members themselves, but also for onlookers. Extreme activists can get caught up in victim status, she argues, and onlookers can develop a sense of overresponsibility and chronic shame. We are all guilty of this, to some extent—both the extremism and the onlooking—because this is how algorithmic life online now works. That is, we can take any tiny sliver of an identity category we fall into and make the argument that we are oppressed—and that empowers onlookers to do the same. Or, on the other hand, an onlooker might feel such sympathy and a codependent-like sense of loyalty and devotion to solving that person's problem because the story and narrative are so compelling that the onlooker gets sucked in, leading to the chronic overresponsibility and shame that Tarico alludes to.

The writing and advocacy of those like Tarico, who are on the ground thinking deeply about the mental and cultural shifts of our era, are vital. There are quiet (and not so quiet) thinkers across all political, religious, and identity spectrums who are beginning to speak openly in more nuanced terms, welcoming diverse people into their folds. Because so many of us feel stuck in self-silencing, there is a sincere craving for such leadership and open-mindedness. But on an individual level—on a layperson level—there is a real psychological crisis on our hands offline, in the day-to-day world. There is no sense of being able to speak freely, whether at school or work (and in some cases even at home). So it's vital to understand what is happening in people's minds.

What Tarico suggests is that the current blind acceptance of anyone's expression of harm or "trauma" as complete unchallengeable fact—as in the case above where a rude coworker claims depression—compared to a more objective acknowledgment of hurt or sad feelings that not everyone else is responsible for, is part of what is plaguing us. Today what dominates are fight-or-flight nervous system states, where a tiny hair trigger becomes full-on fiery war and only absolute surrender is enough to put out the fire. The rude coworker turns to social media to be soothed, and they feel empowered to claim discrimination as a way to avoid the heart of the matter.

Instead of viewing situations from a victim standpoint, Tarico suggests a few helpful reframes for individuals. For example, instead of thinking that one's feelings are the sole reality and that they represent the final truth of a matter without question, she suggests reframing such thinking to "I am not my feelings. My feelings are one indicator of what is real and important, and they are worthy of attention. But they can be wrong or simply out of proportion."

She also suggests that rather than viewing conflict as an attack, we can think to ourselves, "People who respect me will listen to my experiences and self-perceptions but also will challenge me. They will validate my feelings but won't always assume those feelings and the story I am telling myself are the final word on reality." She also suggests that expanding our window of tolerance for being triggered may be an important skill to develop in the face of social media, and especially on college campuses where the point is to challenge one another and learn from different viewpoints. A potential way of thinking might be, "My sense of threat—even getting emotionally flooded—may or may not signal real danger. Trauma causes us to overgeneralize and get triggered by superficial similarities. Staying away from triggers lets the past define me and may make me less resilient. One way to know I am getting healthy is that external people and situations lose their power to trigger me." (Note that while this may not be appropriate in the early months after a genuinely traumatic experience, it's possible that as months go by, and a person experiences more healing, it may be helpful to revise how one thinks of triggers.)

Regarding trauma, she goes further to suggest that bonding over shared trauma can be dangerous and characterizes much of our modern sense of group affiliation. When we limit ourselves to socializing only with those whose ancestors have a shared identity of pain and hardship, we may be limiting our own growth and healing. Her suggested reframe is, "Bad things have happened to my parents and grandparents and me; but they don't have to define me. I do best when I embrace the ways that I can chart my own life."

On the subject of people claiming that only people who have been historically marginalized or oppressed on a large scale can be actual victims today, she is careful and cautious about this way of thinking. People who are victims of past trauma sometimes go on to inflict the same behavior on others, so she suggests staying aware of that reality and switching how we think about trauma and victimhood. "Being a victim doesn't prevent you from victimizing others," she says. "People who harm others very often have experienced similar harms themselves. Often the goal of therapy is to break the cycle."

There is a powerful sense of belonging that comes from banding together under the umbrella of trauma or victimhood. And while this can be vital for initial healing, the goal is not to stay there but rather to find a way out.

Once healing has occurred and people make a shift away from disempowerment toward empowerment and freethinking, they often feel ready to leave the group. This can look like someone from an oppressed group leaving the United States for a long time to explore who they are outside of the confines of

American categories, and it can also look like someone quietly disappearing from "the community" to focus on their career and family and succeed on their own terms away from the victimized group. This might look like simply shifting their focus to everyday life as opposed to constantly spending time with people who reinforce old group narratives and stories. It might also look like diving into material written by the great sages and philosophers as the individual feels ready to expand their outlook on life. Such acts of individuality are often threatening to the group of origin, but ultimately stepping away from the old unifying victim narrative is the key to personal agency, success, and improved mental well-being. It's a challenging process, but incredibly rewarding.

This "stepping away" is what we need more of in our lives, in our media, and in psychology so that we can begin to counter the extremist ways in which outrage-fueled vulnerability and excessive categorization have coalesced to shut freethinkers out, thereby endangering society. The massive danger can only be recognized when you begin to just barely step outside of it or when you begin to subtly notice your own discomfort with the rigid thinking emanating from social media and our self-silencing climate. As Tarico says, "The price of connection is agreement," and as we've already learned, that is not actual connection because it is not based in reality. It is a form of religious belonging based on outrage, tribalism, and extremism.

Tarico, much like the esteemed Columbia University linguist John McWhorter, sees the ways in which political groupthink functions as a religion—and religious thinking or advising does not belong in the secular, therapeutic dynamic between therapist and client. Out in the world, any challenge to groupthink is often seen as heresy, which must be immediately shunned. Any person daring to question must be immediately banished and canceled. Any sanctioned belief is met with tribal support, agreement, and belonging, much like what happens in any cult. So not only does this kind of tribalism not belong in therapy, but such beliefs can also actually create harm. Tarico writes, "These patterns not only trap individuals in depression or conflict, they weaken civil society by feeding mutual mistrust and recrimination, ingroup conformity, outgroup alienation, and widespread cynicism or despair," which is a threat to well-being anywhere, even for people we assume are marginalized and need our help. But people are often wrong with their presumptions about others' supposed groups of belonging, and many people just want to be left alone and live their lives and not be eternally shoved into the artificial shell of a category.

Staying Strong

Research on complexity, creativity, and high intelligence indicates that engaging in complex thinking may set a person up for loneliness in the face of a world that wants us to think according to conventional rules and norms. After all, if a therapist, physician, teacher, or other professional shoves you into a narrow box or category, it can take effort and discipline to not succumb to that same reductionist thinking. It can be tempting to try to fit in with others and black-or-white ways of seeing the world, but if you value being true to yourself, you have probably found that attempting to blend in and accept the status quo makes you miserable and feels impossible. So while we hold on to our authenticity and complexity, know that loneliness will be part of the journey. For me personally, it helps to know some of the research on this and to know that others out there have similar feelings about the importance of integrity, open-mindedness, and critical reasoning.

Lesley Sword and the Gifted Resource Center have found that it's normal for such "gifted" thinkers to:

Have complex and deep thoughts.
Feel intense emotions.
Ask lots of questions.
Be highly sensitive.
Set high standards for themselves.
Have strong moral convictions.
Feel different & out-of-sync.
Be curious.
Have a vivid imagination.
Question rules or authority.
Thrive on challenge.

Additionally, psychologist Mary-Elaine Jacobsen has written in her book, *Liberating Everyday Genius,* that other characteristics include:

Having an insatiable curiosity.
Seeing many sides to nearly any issue.
Prioritizing honesty, integrity, and ethics.
Being a seeker and champion of ultimate truths.
Being very independent.
Seeking out universal truths.
Having an interest in social reform.
Valuing and defending diversity.
Feeling a strong need to make a difference.

Psychologist and author Deirdre Lovecky argues that there are five key traits of gifted thinkers that impact interpersonal relationships. I find these helpful to keep in mind when encountering people who don't value complexity, authenticity, and critical reasoning as much as I do, so I can remind myself of who I am and why social interactions sometimes leave me feeling empty and unfulfilled:

Perceptivity
Sensitivity
Divergency
Excitability
Entelechy

Perceptivity is the quality of being perceptive, *sensitivity* is being acutely attuned to one's environment, *divergency* is the trait of being a divergent thinker and seeing things from multiple angles, *excitability* is a predisposal toward an arousal of intense passion in response to intellectual stimulation, and *entelechy* is the motivating energy or force that drives someone forward in their life.

Of divergency, in particular, Lovecky writes, "A preference for unusual, original, and creative responses is characteristic of divergent thinkers." She continues, "The dilemma of the divergent thinker is one of maintaining identity in the face of pressure to conform. A highly divergent thinker is often a minority of one. If no one else hears the flowers singing, the divergent thinker may experience alienation and eventually an existential depression." I want to briefly comment on depression, specifically, because it is accurate that the ability or desire to engage and communicate in a sophisticated way informed by both emotional insight and critical thinking is rare. We can find ourselves in a struggle to find others who seek the same depth or are capable of the same depth, and that can lead to loneliness. This is yet one more pressure you might find yourself facing when out in the world as a complex thinker. Indeed, many I interviewed for this book felt alienated by society because they dared to think for themselves and then couldn't find as many friends, family members, or colleagues who were comfortable with facing reality in the same way.

On perceptivity, Lovecky writes, "An ability to view several aspects of a situation simultaneously, to understand several layers of self within another, and to see quickly to the core of an issue are characteristic of the trait of perceptivity." In my observation, this kind of perceptivity is often present in folks from a young age. Growing into adulthood, the more one practices developing the skill of critical thought through reflection and conversation with others, the more this perceptivity both heightens and quickens.

The interpersonal implications of being perceptive and being a divergent thinker are thus vast. While some of us are committed to the exchange of truth and critical thought, not everyone shares that goal, especially in a society that is swayed by groupthink. "In fact," Lovecky says of gifted thinkers, "they are often skilled at sensing the incongruency between exhibited social facades and real thoughts and feelings. Another aspect of perceptivity concerns the recognition of and need for truth. Social facades displayed by others may seem to this gifted adult to be a sort of lie. Adults gifted in this way detect and dislike falsehood and hypocrisy."

So, between loneliness, depression, alienation, and pressures to conform, it can feel like the goal of being true to yourself is an uphill battle. It's usually enough to find one or two people who understand you, or you can also look up groups of people who like to gather on these topics, as we will learn about later in the book. It's also vital to take care of other basic needs to support your well-being, like adequate sleep, nutrition, and exercise. But most importantly, from the perspective of connection and belonging, it can be helpful to remember that there are many others out there like you *and* there have been many throughout history—the loners who dare to think differently and produce famous artistic work in the face of pushback or the millions of hidden figures of the past and present who we will never know, who merely sit on park benches or front porches reflecting on the universe. It can be lonely to be a complex thinker. But don't hide. Don't hide your gifts. Don't hide your curiosity. The world needs you, and in the coming chapters we will learn more about individuals and communities dedicated to the cause of authentic expression, dynamic dialogue, and the beauty and freedom of independent thought.

Part III

FINDING CONNECTION

Chapter 7

Debate as the Antidote

Mellessa Denny is an award-winning teacher and debate coach at the high school level in the conservative town of Amarillo, Texas. The students in her debate club come from various backgrounds, and they gather to test out their thinking and communication abilities and to develop friendships and professionally sought-after skills. Denny's husband was recently elected district judge, and they have both navigated complex ideas, situations, and policy questions in their careers and as a couple.

High school debate topics can include everything from minimum age requirements for social media, the ethics of pet ownership, and school uniform requirements to heavier national conversations about injustice, crime, incarceration and forced labor, women's rights, and more. "Debate forces kids to see the other side," Denny tells me. "Especially younger kids, they've never even thought about the flip side of an issue. In the panhandle of Texas, it's real conservative, and the national office does a good job of always trying to find balance so that there's not one side of the issues. We all vote on the debate topics, and students get to vote on national topics as well. And so they try to make sure there's a balance on both sides," she tells me. "A lot of debate coaches tend to be more liberal, but it's not true overall for everyone. Sometimes it depends on rural versus urban areas."

I ask Denny about what debate clubs are like, and "debate culture" in general: Are the kids friends? Do they foster healthy disagreement and challenge one another? "We're blessed in the panhandle of Texas—our kids are friends outside of debate," she tells me. "Soon we'll have tournaments four weekends in a row—they go in shaking hands, wanting to beat each other, but at the end it's just a debate. And I think that happens in most places across the country." She says that the kids respect the fact that some are more conservative or liberal and that there's common ground. Because the spirit of friendship is fostered through debate, they also know it's safe to disagree or have opinions diverge. "And the coaches are the same way," she says. "We're all friends with each other, we know about each other's kids and each other's lives. When you foster the attitude of arguing in a respectful way, then I think it manifests in the debate round, too"—they're being judged after all, and the kids don't want to come across as rude, she adds.

How does one foster an attitude of arguing in a respectful way? It starts with perspective. She tells me about an exercise called *impacting*, where the students are encouraged to think at length about how a policy has a wide range of consequences. Denny sees issues and policies as having "fingers"—that there are many parts to complex problems—and she reminds kids that things are not always as simple as they seem. "Think about the fingers," she tells her students.

Debaters compete in various types of debate rounds, from one-on-one to two-on-two formats. There are judges, who are often members of the community and may range from a community volunteer to a bus driver or firefighter or other local person. Much of the training in debate goes toward encouraging kids to understand and empathize where others are coming from, including the judges they are trying to win over.

After "impacting," Denny has her kids go deep into the "fingers" of an issue, dissecting everything into what she and her class call "nuclear," getting really into all the tiny little details—but then they back off, simplify, and get grounded in order to assess all the information. Students realize that policies do not stand alone and that they affect other issues and communities, she says. For example, on the question of whether school uniforms should be required, students would be reminded that the issue is not limited to freedom of expression, but the more expansive nitty-gritty details might also include the diverse economic makeup of the school and how uniforms take away some of the hierarchy associated with money and access to certain brands or clothing types. The idea is to dive into all aspects of what school uniforms might represent, as well as their impact, so that students can see the topic clearly, think critically about it, and be ready in a debate room.

She also talks with her students about the role of "spin" and how even when there is evidence for something, a person should detect the full extent of the evidence, especially when something is reported in the media. For that purpose, she and her students rely on a website called AllSides to get a "centrist" perspective, as she puts it.

Many students tell her they've never before thought about issues a certain way, and that's what makes debate so important. She reiterates that it's not about changing minds, but understanding what motivates beliefs and the beliefs of others. In doing this work, Denny has also had to interrogate her own views.

"I'm relatively conservative on a lot of things, especially financially, but not so much on social issues like crime and education. I'm a moderate, right in the middle, and it depends on the issue," she tells me when explaining how difficult it is to reconcile one's personal views in theory with actual real life. For Denny, she experienced this challenge in the aftermath of a tragedy.

"I had a student that met someone online, went out with them, and was murdered. Eventually the murderer was convicted. I'm not a big death penalty proponent. I've never been on the side of 'Let's just fry them,'" she continues, mindful of hurrying through the story as it appears painful and yet she wants to share because of the important point she is making.

"When this happened, it was horrifying. And I remember telling my students, 'You know what? Good,'" as she reflected on the death sentence verdict. "And then I thought, 'What?' And so I had to confront something that I had always thought about and how it can sometimes change when it becomes more personal. So we talk about how when it's something we've personally dealt with, it may be harder to understand the other side. We explore what we ourselves have dealt with in our lives and how that directs the way we see things."

She says that even the victim's parents disagreed about whether the death penalty would provide closure for themselves. "We talk with kids about how there's not always a right or wrong answer," she says. "And we explore what's motivating a person to have their opinion in the first place."

Holding Complexity

Former debater and current trainer Zeph Chang wears thick black-rimmed glasses that reflect the bright sunlight from my home in California, in contrast to the overcast weather in the backdrop of his home in Massachusetts. Chang started debate at an early age, saying it helped him feel more confident to speak with strangers, and he went on to place third in the nation and first in Massachusetts. Later he launched a company called Lumos Debate to help students with debate and public speaking skills.

I ask Chang about debate culture in general, and his thoughts on critical reasoning and how society at large can engage more deeply in it. He starts with kids as young as third grade and says he notices that there's a kind of empathy that one develops through debate by seeing many points of view. "Even for young students, when you have questions of minimum wage, welfare, or Medicare, there is a clear sense of, 'Why would we give money for not doing anything?' Or with minimum wage, 'What's the point?' And there's a way in which starting to review evidence, and learning about income inequality and opportunity differences—the switch-side debating is a big part of developing that empathy," he says, referring to the process of debate where students have to prepare both sides of a case before entering a tournament. "When you get to the tournament, at the beginning of every round, there's a coin flip and then you find out if you're debating pro or con."

Chang tells me that debate "really does force students to understand both sides of the argument, and to be able to hold multiple points of view at the same time." I get the sense that this perspective is so normalized in his world that he doesn't realize the specialness of it. So I tell him that and he chuckles. He continues to say that debaters will "give you a very nuanced response, because they've gone into the weeds on both sides." He also adds that that can be good and bad, because young students lose a kind of idealistic conviction or easy black-and-white thinking that is characteristic of youth and naivete.

Then he tells me something profound again. "After you debate a topic, nothing is so clear anymore. And I guess that's the world," he says, to which I respond that this is exactly the frame of mind needed so desperately in the world today, both for personal well-being and for societal functioning. I tell him that learning about the "gray" is a valuable life lesson—and figuring it out well before age forty could save people a lot of grief, in my view. "Yes," he tells me, and "it cuts both ways." He tells me that after a debater goes out into the world and hears people make black-and-white statements, there's a kind of rolling of the eyes that can happen for debaters, and that a sense of innocence or idealism is lost.

Chang used to be extremely shy and was scared to talk to people before high school. Debate gave him the confidence to talk. "Now, so much communication is on the phone. My generation is afraid to call people. Talking in person and eye contact . . . people are just not used to having conversations with strangers." (This is surprising to my millennial self—as a kid who spent most of my youth in conversation with strangers on the San Francisco public transportion system, Muni.)

But debate was a game changer for Chang. He says that students like him "don't realize that they're practicing talking to a person they've never met," because it feels like they're playing a competitive game to win instead, which is a strong motivator for students. He describes debate as dialogue, because you have to try to understand how the judge and competitor think. "It's like a dialogue with somebody who's not talking to you. . . . It forces a kind of empathy—you let go of believing in something 100 percent and think more about where the other person is coming from." He continues, "You have to let go of your ego and what you're holding on to. If you want to change someone's mind, you can't do that by telling them that their core beliefs are completely wrong. You have to work within their framework—ask questions. And the best way to win is to say that everything they say is true," and that within the opponent's belief structure there is room to explore further.

"My observation is that with political discussions my friends are in, they're often about whether X fact is true or not. But usually there is some emotional sentiment coming from both sides that is not actually in contradiction—both sides are worried about X, but the emotions get expressed as truths about the world that become very black or white."

Chang says that his time in debate helped him get out of that kind of thinking.

I get the sense from Chang that debate clubs are exactly what we need more of—the culture, skills, goals, and overall environment offer a splintered society the very tools needed to coalesce. To develop such attributes, there is real work involved—not only the logistics of organizing, coaching, prepping, and debating, but the inner psychological work as well. There's an element of debate that requires "deep work," he says; it's not surface level. He points to the fact that once you start digging into evidence and various studies, you see how poorly some research is carried out, whereas most people just assume any academic study is proof enough of something. Often students will see studies that claim facts almost like a God-given truth, but then you'll find another study that claims just the opposite. "Debate develops a mistrust of authoritative sources that's helpful. Like, there's probably a richer picture there than this one piece of evidence indicates."

Ultimately, being able to firmly hold on to multiple sides engenders a sense of solidity and groundedness in a person, as though they are rooted with many pillars. I think that is a lofty goal for many of us, and for society.

Then Chang utters a final biting statement for our times. "For debaters, it's very rare that the things you believe get tied up with your identity, because you're used to seeing the issue from so many angles." There's less emotional reactivity, and people don't feel threatened by disagreement, he adds. Put simply, embracing disagreement with rigor is the key to our future.

Why Arguing Is Helpful

Studies have shown that experience in debate clubs improves skills like teamwork, listening, and empathy. Contrary to what many believe, debate clubs are powerful forums for every background, not just the well-off. Leading debate educators and speaking coaches AnnMarie Baines, Diana Medina, and Caitlin Healy write in their book, *Amplify Student Voices*, that, "in fact, the structure and facilitation of debate make it safer than some other forms of communication for young people to engage in, because the rules encourage people to listen to different views." Baines is the founder of The Practice Space in the San Francisco Bay Area, where she and her colleagues train children and adults of all backgrounds how to debate, do public speaking, and find their authentic voices. She even gave a recent lecture at the SXSW Conference titled, "We Need to Argue to Heal: How Debate Advances Equity."

According to Baines and her coauthors, the benefits of learning how to speak for oneself and argue in debate formats have lasting effects, including understanding diverse viewpoints, developing empathy and open-mindedness, the ability to challenge fake news, becoming a deliberate listener, learning how to collaborate, and much more. Baines is a nationally recognized speaker and educator who describes herself as once being a quiet Filipina girl who took her first debate class at nine years old and who later went on to volunteer as a debate coach and ultimately graduated from UC Berkeley, Harvard, and the University of Washington and now publishes widely on the topic.

Over in New York, Deanna Kuhn is a leading scholar of critical thinking and a professor at Columbia University; her publications are many, the sound of her voice soft, and her written arguments sharp and cutting. I'm immediately intrigued by her when I stumble on her work, which is vast, and something about her style resonates strongly with me. It is probably because I am a somewhat introverted, sensitive person who has strong opinions and an argumentative side, and I don't often come across others with that particular combination. As it turns out, among many other publications, she is the lead author of a book called *Argue with Me.* While her focus is on education, her insights are widely applicable to society at large in the face of self-silencing and a dearth of independent thinking, because the art of arguing and critical thinking go hand in hand.

"It is in argument that we are likely to find the most significant way in which higher order thinking and reasoning figure in the lives of most people," she writes in the *Harvard Educational Review.* "Thinking as argument is implicated in all of the beliefs people hold, the judgments they make, and the conclusions they come to; it arises every time a significant decision must be made. Hence, argumentative thinking lies at the heart of what we should be concerned about in examining how, and how well, people think," she writes in *Science Education.*

Kuhn's main thesis in her work is that *arguing is thinking,* almost like a constant dialectic between opposing sides or viewpoints; as we think, as we argue, we are iterating repeatedly, constantly, and that is essentially what thought is, in action.

I admire her deep concern that students are not absorbing how to think critically or to question interpretations of those around them. In one of her studies, when she asked students to share their opinions and the evidence for them—and then imagine what someone else's opinion might be on the same issue—she writes, "An average of only 26 percent who did not generate alternative theories offered genuine evidence."

Additionally, about half of her study subjects would be considered absolutists, "who regard knowledge as certain and accumulative," which she describes as shocking. She continues,

> Fully half of a population of average adolescents and adults believe that complex questions, such as why prisoners become repeat offenders, can be answered with complete certainty. Another roughly 35 percent of the sample were classified as multiplists, or relativists. They typically noted that even experts disagree; therefore, nothing is certain, and all opinions are of equal validity. Everyone has a right to their opinion, multiplists maintain, and hence all opinions are equally right. In this way, both absolutists and multiplists leave the knowing process out of their judgments. Only 15 percent of subjects fell into the evaluative epistemological category, in which knowing is regarded as a process that entails thinking, evaluation, and argument.

Such a finding is critical for group exiters, for example, and for developing critical thinking. As Kuhn notes, "This epistemological naïveté may be an important factor in the limited argumentative reasoning ability that people display. People must see the point or the value of argument if they are to engage in it. If one accepts the absolutist view of knowledge as entirely certain and accumulative, or the multiplist view of knowledge as entirely subjective, argument becomes superfluous. Without an epistemological understanding of the value of argument, people may lack the incentive to develop and practice the skills examined here." That is, if individuals are not trained to view knowledge and life as containing constant uncertainties that require reflection and assessment, then people will not see the value in questioning, debating, and arguing because they see the world as containing black-and-white truths or open-ended truths. As I reflect on Kuhn's point, I can say that this understanding is more likely to come later in life with age, and that our world is in dire need of such an understanding at an earlier age, especially as teens and college students spend so much of their lives online, influenced by their peers.

Kuhn, much like debate club coaches and advocates, acknowledges the vital role that social environments play as well. She writes, "Social interaction offers a natural corrective to the egocentrism of individual minds," and she is concerned with how students think, learn, and come to doubt and question in service of arriving at independent conclusions. "The diversity of the social world enhances and corrects individual thought," she writes. "This holds true for the whole range of human discourse, from the simplest everyday conversation to the evolution of scientific theories."

It seems to me that any form of absolutist thinking—from general stubbornness to political ideology to religion—inhibits the ability to develop critical thinking, because rather than being open to new insights, one is constantly shaping one's observations to conform to the worldview that the group or ideology espouses. Kuhn also sees this as a possible barrier, even potentially for debate clubs, but especially for teachers in general. She writes, "The teacher already possesses the understanding of an issue that he or she wishes students to attain. In seemingly 'open' discussion, the teacher shapes students' answers until they finally 'spontaneously' generate the answer the teacher is seeking. Students who 'think well' in such discussions are likely to be those most sensitive to the teacher's communicative cues. Most often missing, even in the best of such 'discovery-based' pedagogies, is genuine, open debate of complex, unanswered questions."

The best teachers model how to think critically and check their biases and ideological convictions at the door. But as viral videos now demonstrate across the political spectrum, teachers are not exempt from the influential force that is social media and the algorithmic focus on categories. While teachers rely on gentle nudging to help students reach certain conclusions, whether in math or English, when it comes to critical thinking exercises, it takes maturity to refrain from nudging, especially toward one's own beliefs.

The Ultimate Debate: Critical Thinking in Schools

Outside of formal speech and debate clubs, there is a raging debate happening within the field of education about how to teach critical thinking (CT). At the core is the question of whether critical thinking should be woven into every class and curriculum implicitly, or if it should be explicitly taught as a stand-alone set of steps and skills, or both. Imagine if you were in a classroom today and either taught an explicit module on the process of critical thinking—with steps listed and all—versus during a history lesson being prompted with a specific exercise about how to think critically about a war, for example, or in an engineering class how to think critically about an environmental challenge. Regardless of approach, there is concern that critical thinking is sorely lacking and that many educators—from professors to middle school teachers—don't know how to teach it. Former Urban Institute researcher Lisa Tsui once wrote that, "while most professors have honed their personal thinking skills, the majority do not possess the pedagogical background to foster them, lack knowledge in balancing the teaching of CT skills with course content, and struggle with the amount of time required to plan appropriately."

Regarding the details of how one might improve their critical thinking, and ways that are being tried in classrooms, the "infusion" approach is one example—also called a "generalist" approach—where critical thinking is woven throughout. The infusion approach, which is implicit, refers to integrating critical thinking skills and instruction into all areas of education, not setting them aside as a distinct unit or subsection of a curriculum. Infusion is thought to be most effective, but results are varied. Being explicit and intentional is also effective—i.e., modeling critical thinking questions, stating out loud that the class is practicing critical thinking, and asking engaging, thought-provoking questions through different mediums, including lectures and interactive videos. "Do you find this convincing, and why or why not? Does this statement's logic raise concerns, and if so, what errors do you see?" are great questions to prompt critical thinking. Likewise, repetition is vital, as is being systematic about the CT instruction. Small group discussions are also helpful in developing, practicing, and reinforcing critical thinking skills. In the *Journal on Centers for Teachers and Learning*, Taylor University associate professor Laura C. Edwards writes, "Discussion seems to be especially effective in teaching higher-order thinking whether professors utilized whole-class or small-group discussions." And modeling—i.e., the professor asking critical questions out loud—has also been found to be effective. The literature indicates that most college students are under-equipped when it comes to critical thinking skills, and there is ample research being done about how to better foster it in classrooms. This is an ongoing challenge for both high school and college instruction.

It's a hot mess, to be honest. There are amazing educators out there, but there lacks a common rigor in fostering open dialogue and a spirit of challenge and constructive argument, which debate clubs seem to counter. We need more classrooms like Mellessa Denny's, but they are rare.

But speaking of what we need more of, I'm often left with a feeling that there is a deeper angle to the education and policy questions—like rather than get fixated on which approach, why don't we consider what studies on the mind and psychology tell us? Or even neurology? I can just imagine leaders in Washington, DC, pulling out psychology studies before deciding on which directions to take, both in education and even in wider political policies like national security or international trade, beyond education.

In a 2020 report from the Education Endowment Foundation (EEF) titled "Metacognition and Self-Regulation: Evidence Review," there is ample discussion about how human minds learn best and what those processes entail. It's important to break the steps down so that you can begin to understand your own mind and conceptualize what is happening throughout your day as you are learning, or when you may be conforming and self-silencing, rather than thinking critically.

Self-regulated learning, for example, refers to taking an active role in setting goals and taking the necessary steps to achieve those goals. Self-regulated learning implies explicit and clear intention, paying attention to one's learning environment, potential distractions, and other factors that impact achieving one's goals. This is an important concept not only for education, but also for all of us out in the world as we curate the people we spend time with, monitor how we structure our lives as it relates to our long-term goals, regulate how we filter information, and more. Self-regulated learning is "a cyclical process" whereby three phases of learning occur: the forethought phase, which is what is going on in our minds before engaging in a learning task (e.g., preparing to set out to read a book), the performance phase (the encoding of information in our brains as we are reading the book), and the self-reflection phase (what we synthesize and process after we finish reading).

This concept of self-regulated learning plays out throughout our days when we browse the grocery store aisles, take in all the information, and carefully decide what our hands will pick up or how we handle an interruption when a store clerk speaks to us. We need to stay on task; otherwise, we will forget or spend far too long at the store. Likewise, self-regulated learning occurs when we attend spiritual gatherings and must monitor and manage what information we want to integrate and what information is unhelpful to us. Self-regulated learning is a constant process.

Part of self-regulated learning is metacognition, which "can be seen as the instructions we give ourselves on how to do a particular learning activity or task, while cognition is the way we actually do them. Metacognition then returns as the monitoring of the success of these activities," the EEF report continues. How well did you handle yourself while attending that new atheist meeting, where you weren't so sure you agreed with the group and had to be intentional about both the learning of new information and about evaluating how well you resisted self-silencing in the face of the information and people in the group?

What I appreciate about discussions behind metacognition and self-regulated learning is that they imply an "active" poise on the part of the individual. For example, having to define tasks, plan and set goals, deploy attention, and modulate responses all assume an active, engaged person. This is an empowering stance and implies the opposite of the more passive, victim, ideological, or overly devoted poise awaiting instruction. "Modelling by adults is a key way in which children develop self-regulation, and teachers can successfully demonstrate and model (context-specific) metacognitive strategies," according to the EEF report. Outside of the classroom, beyond teachers, I think parents, neighbors, mentors, librarians, and even politicians could play this role, too, helping to model more intentional ways of learning and staying engaged.

When debate clubs come together, it seems there is also a process of social metacognition in place—a phenomenon also referred to as *socially shared regulation of learning* (SSRL). Beyond mere group work, this term describes the internal and external processes among people when the skills and tools of metacognition come together with multiple people. It's a powerful concept because when strong metacognition is in place among several people, there is enormous potential for in-depth learning and perspective shifting to happen. One could say that a culture is almost created—a culture where minds are open and agile and ready to change viewpoints when authentically convinced. With the debate coaches I interviewed, there was a common value placed on being able to see all sides of a policy, for example.

There remains in our society an issue of modeling and instruction, however, and it seems making speech and debate a school requirement would go a long way in aiding the development of strong metacognition. The EEF authors write, "Most students develop metacognition spontaneously, picking it up from their parents, peers, and teachers, but there is considerable variation between students in their level of metacognition, and a relatively large group of students does not acquire a sufficient level of metacognition, due to a lack of opportunities, role models, or effort put into acquiring it."

Once again, research finds that immersion and explicit modeling are essential, with potential to impact settings beyond education as well. Teachers and schools are good starting points, but we need news anchors, professors, influencers, librarians, parents, journalists, YouTubers, and many more members of society to help combat the dearth of independent thinking skills in our world today. There is implicit modeling, for example, where a professor or news anchor might verbalize their internal thought process, and then explicit modeling where the speaker will announce aloud that she is "modeling a learning strategy" so that students or viewers are intentionally aware. In educational settings, "cognitive apprenticeship" (CA) is also effective, which involves scaffolding, coaching, articulation, and reflection. Research also shows that metacognitive reflection is most effective *after* task completion, as "task competition needs to fully engage cognition," according to the EEF report. All of this research on various approaches is enlightening when it comes to learning to think, question one's thinking, improve one's critical thinking, and live day-to-day life in the world as a robust independent thinker.

By getting granular—especially for those of us who do not work in the field of education—we can reflect on what we might have missed out on in our own early education and then proceed to fill in the gaps with these new insights about honing critical reasoning. In other words, we can all learn to overcome self-silencing and groupthink by being intentional about how we learn, where we acquire information from, and the settings we immerse ourselves in. For example, since modeling can be helpful for learning, what environments or websites or teachers can you seek out that will model independent thinking? Like a diet where you are choosing foods to add and other foods to take out, we can all do the same when it comes to our minds. We can make choices every day—from the friends we surround ourselves with to the social media apps we use—that empower us to be conscious individual thinkers.

Beyond Clubs and Classrooms

I must admit some vulnerability here in that I am uncertain about the limits and power of independent thinking on its own as opposed to the spirit of group rebellion that can spawn generational change and growth. I champion how people challenge power and create new ways of being in the world, but I worry that what some think is their own individual thought and expression is actually rhetoric that is desperately reinforced by lobbying entities that rely on the narrative of marginalization to secure votes. If individuals are constantly categorized according to one feature, painted as a monolith, and are the recipients of constant messaging imparting one particular point of view that supposedly represents themselves, it becomes increasingly difficult to break out of that way of thinking. In individual moments it's not always clear what is coming from the individual versus the group, but that is part of the dance of critical thinking—constant gut checks, questioning oneself, and speaking boldly help us move forward confidently in the world.

Critical reasoning is a complex skill, and as I scoured the internet for commentary on the subject, I stumbled upon a former West Point student's master's paper that argued that critical thinking is "a relatively unnatural, higher order skill." It's not supposed to be easy and involves the very ability to hold complexity that debater Zeph Chang so brilliantly alludes to. Simple shifts can help. "Simply shifting to a new medium can help disrupt a tendency for students to be passive observers in the classroom," the paper argues, and to me this echoes the dangers of social media: If we're all glued to our phones, it becomes routine, desensitizing us to self-silencing culture, both in what we observe in others and in what is happening inside our own selves.

One angle to consider is the kinds of minds who are already working a little differently from the mainstream and what they might have to offer in seeing problems differently. Many "neurodivergent" people are accustomed to living at the margins by virtue of how they think. We are used to being alone, often sensing or realizing a phenomenon is occurring well before others. We pick up on patterns, and many neurodivergent people, by virtue of their mind makeup, crave nuance. They crave nuance while at the same time loving rules—as long as those rules make sense. Neurodivergents feel a strong need to understand, and a need to ask questions and discuss at length. This is debate culture, but it's also neurodivergent culture.

In fact, I wasn't surprised to learn that the author of the viral *New York Times* op-ed about censorship, Emma Camp, who we met in chapter 1, was not only a University of Virginia senior on the autism spectrum but that she was also heavily involved in her campus's debate club. Chatting over Zoom with her was refreshing as we got to discuss both free speech and neurological diversity. I wanted to hear more of her own personal story: Was this critical reasoning bug always in her? Was it shaped by her parents? Did it have to do with her autism?

"I grew up in rural Alabama," she starts off. "I lived in a town that was very conservative, and quite diverse. My parents were the only Democrats I knew for a long time." She remembers watching Rachel Maddow with her parents from a young age and arguing with classmates about ObamaCare in third grade. "I remember feeling pressure to not say anything from a young age, but not backing down, and also learning to get along with others. I had to get along with people who believed very different things from me, as my parents were not very religious amidst a very religious community. I was the only one who didn't go to a church." That was formative for her, and it set the tone for her life.

Her parents were college educated, but other parents in the community were steel mill workers, for example, who had not attended college. And growing up amid so much contrast ultimately made her a sharp observer of human diversity. "I ended up going to a fine arts high school in Alabama, so that was a liberal oasis in a conservative state, but I think in terms of my interest in free speech, I'm not entirely sure where it comes from."

She had been bored in school, as the schools in the area were underfunded and didn't have great reputations for high-quality education. At the time, her parents didn't have the money for private school or to move. But things changed when they divorced when Emma was fourteen and she and her brother went to new schools because their new stepdad had enough money to live in an area where the schools were better funded. In that new neighborhood, she realized that where she had been prior was not in fact an accurate representation of the population. "I was under the impression until early high school that half the American population was Black," she says. And when she moved to the "ritzy suburb," it was noticeable how white it was. They were both conservative neighborhoods, however, despite the racial and class differences. And as we're chatting, I'm nodding because somehow, across the US, her experience was very similar to my own, growing up in heavily multi-racial environments and thinking that was standard. And like me, she doesn't know whether the neurodivergence informed her heterodox orientation to nuanced discourse or whether it was her unique upbringing immersed in political and economic diversity that made her so comfortable with disagreement and dialogue.

"One of the best things to happen to me was college debate club," she says immediately. "The best way to describe it is people that like talking about weird things coming together and having meetings on Fridays where people give little speeches and presentations on everything from cricket to midterms to poetry."

She says that the people who are attracted to the debate club on her former college campus of University of Virginia are a specific type, and that has formed her primary friend circle. Those friendships have continued beyond graduation into her new city of Washington, DC. "It was so uniquely embracing of ideological diversity," she says of the club and friend group. "Being able to talk about whatever and still be friends with someone when you have really big gaps in what you believe—I find that to be very rich that I can be friends with someone who thinks radically different from me."

Emma shares something poignant with me in that she says, while she's seen what can go drastically wrong when it comes to censorship and speech, she's also been in settings where free speech is so beautifully welcomed and embraced. "I'm someone who historically has struggled to make friends. I didn't really have friends until I went to college." She adds that even though she went to an arts high school, she was "too weird for the weird school" and that she just didn't fit in. "I'm very passionate about things and I have an innate earnestness that is generally not in vogue, especially among teenagers. So finding a place where caring about something is what makes you cool, and where you're encouraged to pursue your special interest and then make a presentation for forty-five minutes—that was one of the best things to ever happen to me and something I'm really, really grateful for."

Finally, she reiterates that a lot of the censorship concerns on campus stem from bad university policies and "overeager administrations to censor," which is such a sharp contrast to the debate coaches and clubs we've heard from so far, offering even more reason why debate culture and dissent are vital to our society and our well-being. As she puts it, "If you're afraid of being caught saying the wrong thing, you're necessarily afraid of thinking the wrong thing."

Whether at a university, a psychologist's office, or at home, when strict rules are imposed on how to act or what to say (or not say), many of us start to feel squirmy, like something isn't right. And part of ending self-silencing culture is noticing that discomfort more and more within oneself. We must implement the necessary resources and structures that foster debate, critical reasoning, and empathetic communication, instead of blanket censorship policies.

There are also those who don't care to engage in the culture wars. Out in the field of everyday real life, there are thousands of caring, thinking individuals who don't have the interest or luxury of time to dwell, process, and analyze about niche topics. Caregivers, doctors, parents, football coaches, and countless others are living their lives, enjoying their families and communities, enduring life's natural struggles, and they are able to have balanced conversations at the dinner table or in break rooms at work.

There are also the individuals whose job it is to help steer our society toward a healthier relationship with media, politics, and debate: A whole host of notable thinkers, writers, and journalists are beginning to coalesce into not so much a "group," but a woven thread helping others to see that critical dissent is fun, healthy, and productive. While at times controversial, UnHerd and Compact are examples of smaller publications that push back against both left and right dogmatism, and writers such as Sarah Haider, Erec Smith, and Sheena Mason all have created Substacks where they discuss nuanced topics from an informed, critical perspective. These outlets have become places for people to share openly, away from fear, and engage in healthy dialogue and debate. The expansion of viewpoint diversity across multiple spheres of life doesn't only help us tolerate disagreement better. When we cultivate the capacity for healthy friction, we also make it easier to connect with one another, eschew performativity, and communicate from a place of sincere curiosity.

Chapter 8

Embracing Our Depth

In the middle of writing this book, I felt something off in my close examination of self-silencing and free expression. While the values of liberty and independent thought sit close to my heart, there are others as well, namely family and friendship. I knew that love, and true belonging, somehow figured into the picture, but how?

Along with the sacredness of the individual, there is also a sacredness in relationality—that is, in the intimate bonds we form with those of our choosing, whether it's a partner, best friend, or even an animal. If we only focus on developing our own gifts—and never learn to share them, compromise, or experience the beauty of overcoming tension and conflict—we are somehow less whole. I know that is a bold statement, but it is true. This doesn't mean that you can't accomplish wholeness on your own, but you must allow yourself to be burned, to test the waters, to engulf yourself in the flames of relational challenges—real-life, in-person challenges, not the faux world of social media.

This is not a book about love or relationships or trauma; it is about how to be one's own person among a crowd—but that doesn't always mean remaining *separate* from the crowd. Our goal as human beings should be to fully develop ourselves both as individuals and as community members—whether it's a community of two or two thousand.

So, I wanted to better understand what is happening to friendships, relationships, colleagues, and neighbors. Has social media siloed us beyond repair? Does our perception of polarization cloud our ability to communicate at ease? Is the perception of heightened tension itself a trick of social media?

In my view, from interviewing and observing others, our boundaries for what is acceptable have become smaller. Basic human mistakes are grounds for cutting people off, reducing the size of our social circles and deeper friendships. Trust is given to a rare few. The way we evaluate our own selves is worse because every interaction is measured in the currency of likes and shares. It seems we need an evolution of forgiveness with online interactions, but that needs to translate to forgiving ourselves and each other in real offline life as well. But forgiveness starts with facing reality, being realistic about human nature, and leading our lives with integrity.

Friendship and Authenticity

In the 2023 publication of the *Routledge Handbook of Philosophy of Disagreement,* referencing the philosopher John Locke's ideas, writers Sebastien Bishop and Robert Mark Simpson write, "We let people hold onto their own ethical convictions, and, rather than weakening the sovereign's ability to maintain the peace, this actually results in a more resilient form of unity." We must practice the ability to sit with difference, accept it, perhaps even enjoy it, and then move on with our day. "Disagreement is dangerous in principle, but we can achieve an armistice, in the war of all against all, by letting people hold their own convictions, and by cultivating a tolerant ethos that breeds solidarity in the face of difference," they write.

Where Locke was cautious yet optimistic about the healthy role of disagreement, the philosopher John Stuart Mill embraced the *productivity* of disagreement—not only for society, but for individuals in coming to their own conclusions in the process of disagreeing. Referencing Mill's ideas, Bishop and Simpson write, "We need an environment in which we encounter disagreement and diversity, in ideas and in lifestyles, so that we are inspired to resist conformity and live our own way." Individuality was central to Mill's view of well-being and human flourishing, and he viewed disagreement as containing vital "generative potential" that allows for "positive intellectual friction."

Indeed, Mill thought that by protecting free speech, "we ensure that society will be too intellectually turbulent for dogmatism to set in, and thus we guard against a major threat to mental vitality." I'd argue that free speech also protects against the loss of *relational* vitality—in friendships, classrooms, and beyond. I think the inability to tolerate and embrace diversity of ideas more broadly in society translates directly into the quality of our friendships. Without the friction of debate and disagreement, our relationships lack vigor.

There is an enticing dance, an "intellectual party," so to speak, that erupts when people from all walks of life enter a room together. Many people mourn the loss of this as it has become more difficult to encounter, not only in regular life but on campuses and online. We must work to preserve the vibrancy of debate even, or especially, within close friendships. How is this done? How do people develop the skill to befriend difference, to sit with it, accept it—and even, perhaps, to love it?

In her article, "The Speech Gods: Freedom of Speech, Censorship, and Cancel Culture in the Age of Social Media," legal studies professor Kathleen Hidy writes, "In a free and democratic society, diversity of thought is buttressed through the freedom to engage in reasoned discourse, debate, and dissent." A crucial part of such engagement is knowing how to listen—and to really hear others. As we know, the slow process of active listening is vital for friendships, society, and sustained social change. Active listening implies an extremely engaged way of paying attention, interacting, and hearing another person. It involves paying attention to body cues, not interrupting, and refraining from planning what to say next. It also involves repeating the other person, checking for accuracy, and then taking time to thoughtfully respond. It is a challenging endeavor because it's a far cry from much of the fast-paced communication styles that dominate, but it leads to deeper understanding between people.

The understanding that can come out of active listening as opposed to a combative or narrow-minded response has the potential to create a bridge between seemingly opposing forces. This can be useful in one-off situations where conflicting perspectives collide, but even greater potential lies in the bonds that might form if we brought this type of attention and open-mindedness to long-term relationships. The celebrated liberal author and professor Cornel West, for example, has a longstanding close friendship with Princeton professor Robert P. George, who is conservative. The two are often seen hugging and joking during media interviews, and their friendship is an excellent model for preserving integrity and respect in a close relationship across various forms of difference. The two even developed a petition that has now been signed by thousands of professors. Below is their joint statement, titled "Truth Seeking, Democracy, and Freedom of Thought and Expression":

> The pursuit of knowledge and the maintenance of a free and democratic society require the cultivation and

practice of the virtues of intellectual humility, openness of mind, and, above all, love of truth. These virtues will manifest themselves and be strengthened by one's willingness to listen attentively and respectfully to intelligent people who challenge one's beliefs and who represent causes one disagrees with and points of view one does not share.

That's why all of us should seek respectfully to engage with people who challenge our views. And we should oppose efforts to silence those with whom we disagree—especially on college and university campuses. As John Stuart Mill taught, a recognition of the possibility that we may be in error is a good reason to listen to and honestly consider—and not merely to tolerate grudgingly—points of view that we do not share, and even perspectives that we find shocking or scandalous. What's more, as Mill noted, even if one happens to be right about this or that disputed matter, seriously and respectfully engaging people who disagree will deepen one's understanding of the truth and sharpen one's ability to defend it.

None of us is infallible. Whether you are a person of the left, the right, or the center, there are reasonable people of goodwill who do not share your fundamental convictions. This does not mean that all opinions are equally valid or that all speakers are equally worth listening to. It certainly does not mean that there is no truth to be discovered. Nor does it mean that you are necessarily wrong. But they are not necessarily wrong either. So someone who has not fallen into the idolatry of worshiping his or her own opinions and loving them above truth itself will want to listen to people who see things differently in order to learn what considerations—evidence, reasons, arguments—led them to a place different from where one happens, at least for now, to find oneself.

All of us should be willing—even eager—to engage with anyone who is prepared to do business in the currency of truth-seeking discourse by offering reasons, marshaling evidence, and making arguments. The more important the subject under discussion, the more willing we should be to listen and engage—especially if the person with whom we are in conversation will challenge our deeply held—even our most cherished and identity-forming—beliefs.

It is all-too-common these days for people to try to immunize from criticism opinions that happen to be dominant in their particular communities. Sometimes this is done by questioning the motives and thus stigmatizing those who dissent from prevailing opinions; or by disrupting their presentations; or by demanding that they be excluded from campus or, if they have already been invited, disinvited. Sometimes students and faculty members turn their backs on speakers whose opinions they don't like or simply walk out and refuse to listen to those whose convictions offend their values. Of course, the right to peacefully protest, including

> on campuses, is sacrosanct. But before exercising that right, each of us should ask: Might it not be better to listen respectfully and try to learn from a speaker with whom I disagree? Might it better serve the cause of truth-seeking to engage the speaker in frank civil discussion?
>
> Our willingness to listen to and respectfully engage those with whom we disagree (especially about matters of profound importance) contributes vitally to the maintenance of a milieu in which people feel free to speak their minds, consider unpopular positions, and explore lines of argument that may undercut established ways of thinking. Such an ethos protects us against dogmatism and groupthink, both of which are toxic to the health of academic communities and to the functioning of democracies.

In another collaborative media piece, in conversation with Stanford professor Francis Fukuyama and others, West shares, "All the talk about plurality and diversity and equity and all these bureaucratic categories trying to deal with difference—when it really comes down to it, this class doesn't respect ordinary people. So this multiculturalism within the professional-managerial class, what does it do? It just makes the empire more colorful. It just makes class hierarchy more colorful. And yet the damage is still done—people still feel as if they're pushed to the margins, as if their dignity is being crushed."

In a study of almost five thousand high schoolers in the United States, researchers Siwei Cheng and Yu Xie found that "increased context size promotes racial segregation and discourages interracial friendship," by which they mean the larger the school size, the more segregated the groups become. This is found in other studies as well, and points to the importance of micro-groups and communities—that is, finding associations in smaller diverse groups where in-depth exposure across difference may lead to less self-segregating in everyday life and the fostering of authentic friendships. In other words, people need more practice—more exposure—from a young age so that an "unfamiliar" person doesn't remain a distanced "other" in high school and beyond.

According to researchers Young Kim et al. in *Research in Higher Education*, "Interracial friendship is associated with a number of favorable outcomes including positive feelings towards other racial/ethnic groups, prejudice reduction, and access to non-redundant information." They continue, however, that "in 2004, only 15 percent of US adults reported having a friend of another race with whom they discussed important matters. Prior to adulthood and before coming to college, residential and school segregation are major blocks to interracial friendship for students." They conclude that "interracial friendship in college is directly impacted by interracial friendship in high school, which in turn is affected by the racial diversity of a student's high school. While there is always an element of choice in friendship, our findings remind us of how friendship is shaped by more than personal preference;

college and pre-college socialization in different types of environments also matter." That is, the earlier the exposure the better, which should prompt all of us to think about how our choice of where to live or send our kids to school will ultimately affect our own friendships and exposure to difference, as well as our families'.

According to research appearing in the *Journal of Social Issues* by a leading group of social scientists in Canada and the United States, constantly anticipating race-based rejection is a source of chronic stress, but having interracial friendships eases this stress. They write in their findings that people with friends across different racial groups are more familiar with interracial contexts and have developed "social skills" for such settings. And given more ease, familiarity, and positive experiences, such friendships can help reduce any hesitance or uncertainty about "intergroup interactions." Finally, they write that people more familiar with interracial friendships are more likely to seek social support across racial lines following any kind of interracial conflict, which represents a coping strategy that might help blunt future conflict that arises in cross-racial settings. That is, by having interracial friendships, people gain more positive associations regarding interracial friendships, which then leads to more feelings of connection and trust. When any potential interracial conflict may arise in other areas of a person's life, they have friends to turn to across racial lines, which also helps reduce the negative effects of interracial conflict, because the positive association is present from the other existing interracial friendships.

Their research scope was simple: Those who *expect* negative experiences from interracial contexts, like danger or rejection, might perceive interracial dynamics or friendships to be daunting or demanding. But the people who already have more familiarity and experience with interracial contexts feel prepared to navigate interracial settings. They write, "By its definition, cross-race friendship involves intimate, cooperative interracial interactions, which, when repeated over time, should extinguish learned associations between outgroup members and race-based rejection. . . . Overall, then, the pattern of findings suggest that cross-race friendship is especially beneficial for people who have negative expectations of outgroup members."

Astoundingly, they summarize their findings as follows:

> The present research is the first to find that people who are more likely to feel anxious about interracial interactions show signs of more chronic burdens of stress (i.e., stress symptoms) when they have fewer coping resources, such as social support from different race friends. As with the work on acute stress, the present findings also speak to the power of close relationships that cross racial boundaries. People who were predisposed to experience stress in interracial contexts exhibited fewer daily psychosomatic symptoms after making a cross-race friend in the lab. Altogether, this work shows that psychosocial factors related to stress and coping in interracial contexts affect daily psychosomatic symptomatology in nuanced

> ways. . . . The chronic, uncontrollable possibility of race-based rejection in diverse societies may predispose some people to appraise diverse contexts as stressful, but only when resources for coping with this stress are low. . . . We present cross-race friendship as a pathway through which diversity can lead to physiological thriving.

What the study means for communities and individuals is that friendship across difference actually improves perceptions of one another and reduces stress. Knowing that you have someone to turn to improves your physiological response to potentially stressful situations. In other words, connecting across difference improves your health. So, as you seek to show up more authentically in the world, reduce self-silencing, and get more comfortable with diversity of viewpoint, know that there is power in actively choosing who you surround yourself with and that those choices have the power to improve your overall well-being.

Fighting in Love, and in War

I often think of our current polarization as a high-conflict, mismatched married couple. Imagine one partner has been marginalized due to a status difference—that is, perhaps they are not as wealthy as their partner. But the marginalized partner eventually earns an education and a high-paying job, and so they feel empowered by their newfound access to knowledge and resources. The conundrum, then, is how do the two partners allow for this status shift, this identity transition? In this particular case, studies show that the partner who started out with the lower income would have built up feelings of powerlessness and shame over time. So when there is suddenly equal power, there are new rules to be negotiated in terms of who makes decisions, how to communicate about finances, and more.

Expanding this idea outward, when considering the pursuit of equality and power among groups who have been marginalized, we must ask how this same dance plays out on a worldwide scale. The hard-core activists of X, for example—God bless them—*demand* change, and I respect their fiery spirit. There are, however, other individuals and advocates on X who turn to more philosophical approaches to change; they prefer to slowly tease out the nuance of emerging sociocultural and political dynamics. Both approaches represent what the hypothetical marginalized partner might do—one strategy to reach power is fast, breaking down walls, and the other is reflective and methodical and, some might say, more sustainable.

But there's a third option, where there is room for both. And I think there *is* room for both because each approach accomplishes different means. The activist approach puts immediate needs front and center, and the slower philosophical approach prioritizes careful, nuanced inquiry. It seems to me that one group can be working on one project while the other works on another. In that way, change is efficient.

But there has been very little room for the slower philosophical types to be seen and heard in the culture wars. There is little education around such things as viewpoint diversity, political diversity, or even the diverse value systems *within* various groups to begin with. There is no single story or "representation."

Survival Psychology

I also think that part of being a good friend, community member, and citizen is having a *solid grasp on reality*. When people are distracted by ideology, it's difficult to relate to others human to human.

A lot of emotion is subtle, for example, and subtlety is hard. Do you find it easier to lash out in anger, or to actually sit there and face someone who has hurt you and tell them how sad they made you? For most people, anger is the easier route. It's impulsive, undisciplined, and feels like a "release" in the moment. But it's a cover. The sadness underneath is actually harder to sit with and requires more skill, a skill we as people lack. Our digital habits only worsen this feeling, where a tiny hair trigger sets off a fight-or-flight nervous system response and becomes a full-on fiery war.

It's very possible that what many think is vulnerability—especially the rage and outrage culture of social media—actually is not. People merely scratch at the surface and don't get to the harder (sadder, vulnerable) parts. This false sense of vulnerability fueled by anger and rage—which is a form of what I'll call "fake depth"—is also what gives rise to cancel culture and why it feels (supposedly) good to lash out online. The undisciplined and unguided impulses of the masses on social media is a communication disaster.

However, there is a universal shared experience we can all draw on that helps temper our emotions, grounding us in the reality of the human experience of being confined to our bodies and what that entails: hunger, illness, survival, death.

To this end, I became curious about *survival psychology*, much of it grassroots knowledge stemming from literal survivalists—those who spend extensive lengths of time out in the wilderness. Survival psychology is the psychology of surviving in extreme environments, usually outdoors, and implies the inner strategies, mindsets, and ways of thinking that help people survive. Another way of thinking about this small area of study is the study of embodiment: To truly capture the body's goal in this world boils down to one word, *survival*, and examining ways of survival in extreme environments helps clarify how individuals can better face reality in all circumstances of life, on a daily level, not just in extreme situations. Psychologist Kathy McMahon and author Laurence Gonzales both write on such topics, including the importance of collecting information about one's environment for survival, being clear-headed and avoiding confusion and hesitation when in dangerous environments, staying humble, and avoiding self-pity. These sound surprisingly similar to how to become resilient, avoid overidentifying with being a victim, and engage in more deliberate communication and action.

McMahon expands on what to actually do in acute danger, which can be applied to life more broadly, but also how to survive under mass groupthink, which is a kind of existentially dangerous environment. She emphasizes intentionally facing the situation, staying calm, using humor, getting organized by planning out required tasks to survive, taking bold action, celebrating small wins, being grateful, incorporating play, staying hopeful about success and survival, putting fear aside, having a strong will, and never giving up.

This all translates to facing disagreement in real time and learning how to better counter those in front of you who may challenge you. Staying centered, wise, and grounded while engaging in critical debate is vital, and is an act of existential survival so you don't wilt in the face of pressure to conform. Breathing and relying on our bodies is helpful, if you are inclined to put your hand on your chest, for example. Others are great at easing tension through humor. Others still are methodical thinkers and like to prepare by making lists of options, like "We have three options, A, B, or C. Let's start there." As McMahon explains in the context of survival psychology, it's important to not let go and not give up. Perhaps you and your family can release tension by playing football in the backyard or taking a brisk walk, and then come back to the dinner table to discuss Christmas plans. Either way, getting through hard conversations requires staying aware, getting grounded, thinking through options, and communicating in hopeful ways so as to ease the nervous systems of those around you. "We will survive this!" might be a literal mantra to hold in your mind in tense situations.

Such tips also remind me of the psychologist Marlene Winell's steps for recovering from religious extremism. Her steps of religious recovery are:

Get real.

Get a grip.

Get informed.

Get help.

Get a life.

Get with the program.

Get your groove on.

Moving away from the stronghold of groupthink requires centering yourself in your body and the present moment in a deep way. And by that I mean maintaining a deep confidence born from your brave journey of questioning that brought you to this moment where your authentic internal change of perspective is now being challenged from the outside. Getting real, maintaining a grip, communicating to others, and moving forward with your life are brave existential survival acts.

Both everyday conflicts and survival psychology require a dedication to facing reality, moving boldly, and staying steadfast with hope. For former prisoners of war, commentators refer to the threat of what they call "give-up-itis (GUI)" in moments of acute danger. Writer Kyle Howington describes GUI as social and behavioral withdrawal, a "noticeable degree of apathy," "loss of willpower, emotional responsiveness, and an ability to act decisively," nonresponse to external stimuli, and psychogenic death. The antidote to GUI, Howington suggests, is hope. Hope is absolutely essential to staying alive when enduring crises of survival. He writes, "You must always be prepared to adapt to an unexpected environment while having the ability to develop effective coping mechanisms to maintain hope." All of this reminds me of what is required to existentially survive and stay on one's feet, harnessing the agility necessary to face the challenge of groupthink with critical dissent. By honing survival skills, your emotional backbone grows and you become firmer in who you are and more poised to survive—effectively becoming a stable source of strength, insight, wisdom, perseverance, calm, and rationality. And by becoming a more grounded person, you are also more poised to connect with others from a healthy place.

Refraining from getting sucked into scrolling on social media and flooding your body with outrage, for example, requires discernment and restraint, two traits needed when surviving out in the wild. There are whole movements now centered around "tech sabbaths," where individuals and families turn off their devices for twenty-four hours from sundown Friday to sundown Saturday. The Unplug Collaborative organizes the Global Day of Unplugging, helping to turn cities into "unplugged villages" and the organization encourages activities like origami, riding bikes, dancing, decluttering, baking, blowing bubbles, and numerous others. Unplugging, embracing play, and "touching grass" all help develop our ability to relate to others in real time, relearning patience as opposed to the instant gratification of messaging apps or social media likes, and we ultimately become more tolerant as we remember what it means to be human and acknowledge each other's humanity.

Another part of being human is learning the art of forgiveness, which also requires agility, facing reality, discernment, and forthrightness, all essential for survival as well, and which demand being honest about the situations we find ourselves in. Researchers on forgiveness repeatedly show that admitting and accepting our mistakes is vital for moving forward and forgiving ourselves. Facing reality helps us survive and helps us heal.

There is a common thread throughout, between survival psychology, religious recovery, exiting cults, and embodiment. They all center on the process of coming home to one's body and getting grounded in the real and now, which allows for a person to tap into what they really think, what their viewpoints, opinions, and decisions are, and what they want to say and do in the world. In other words, knowing what you think and being able to verbalize it and act on it, is a form of existential survival in the face of overwhelming pressure to censor and self-silence.

Converging Dialogues: Approaching Difference with Calm Forgiveness

Xavier Bonilla started his podcast, *Converging Dialogues*, during the pandemic after friends and colleagues encouraged him to do so. He set aside one weekend and bought a bunch of equipment and set out to talk to a wide array of people with diverse viewpoints. "I wanted to have conversations with everybody and get different points of view," he tells me. A laid-back yet sharp-thinking psychologist with tattoos covering both arms, he shares that ever since he was a kid he was interested in people and how they think and interact with one another. He's "very interested in humans," he says. He disagrees with his guests all the time, but he stays friendly.

> One of my most formative memories is the first time I went to my dad's country, El Salvador, just after the civil war ended there. I was a kid, so it was cool to get on a plane and see people in a completely different place. . . . There was extreme poverty and they had just had a war, so it was still tough, but it left an imprint on me. And then a couple years later I took a road trip with my uncle across the United States and I saw people from all over. And so you start to see that people are the same everywhere. So I always knew that I wanted to be around different kinds of people.

I point out to Bonilla that these insights are somewhat of a rarity—not so much the desire to connect, but the fact that he was exposed to wide differences early on and that he seized his early experiences to cultivate even more curiosity and exposure. I relate to this, and in fact many people in the heterodox space have a similar story of early exposures to difference that created a kind of baseline normalcy for them. Bonilla is humble about it, but I point out that it's in fact not normal for many.

He also tells me that he's a secular humanist, and he describes that orientation as having "no bottom to the well," meaning that he has an almost endless empathy and compassion for human beings, even when they do harm. "I believe very strongly in a kind of forgiveness or redemptive piece to the picture. People are really complicated, and we're really messy."

I ask how he feels being part of the media now, since his primary work is as a psychologist in private practice. Is he afraid of saying the wrong thing publicly? Is he afraid of being canceled? "I'm aware that if I write something or say something publicly, I have responsibility for myself to be as prudent as possible with the things I say. I'm going to get ideas wrong or I might speak extemporaneously and say something not right, but I put forth my very best effort in every conversation to be very mindful of what I'm saying," he says.

When asked about his advice for other emerging public thinkers, he describes his tips as "two connected heuristics." First, he says that "not everything needs to be an eleven," and what he means is that even when there is an issue or cause you care about, you don't need to remain in high-stakes panic mode about it all the time. The second thing is that it's a good idea to take a day off from focusing on that issue constantly. "We have to have robust life experiences," and not get so caught up in an obsessive issue all day every day. He cites tennis and books as examples that keep him balanced, for example. "Each issue should have a ceiling, either for that day or week, and we should fill our minds with other things or just be more present. And I think if people did these things, things would be a lot better and less reactionary."

"At the end of the day, as long as we take responsibility for our words and our actions as best we can, be mindful and forgiving of ourselves and other people's mistakes, and keep the humanity of others central—and not everything at an eleven—I think that could make things a little bit better."

Reconnecting with our physical presence—our own bodies and the world around us, beyond our phones—helps keep our thinking sharp, because our perceptions are more connected to a full-body lived experience than to floating words across a screen. Sometimes shifting attention from words to our physical selves can be a challenge for introspective thinkers because we value quiet thought and insight. But as we journey further into thinking and living critically, we realize that staying glued to the world around us *is* the intelligent choice. Taking breaks for walks, exercise, sport, travel, tea, and other "real world" enjoyment shuffles our senses and perceptions and fuels us as we journey onward.

Chapter 9

The Power of Comedy

What exactly helps individuals bounce back from hurt feelings? In other words, if I go about my life taking random jokes in stride, what enables me to do that? What are the micro components of my emotional backbone that fortify me in confidence, optimism, joy, and humor that allow me to take a quick hit and push back with a bit of laughter?

There is a whole science of comedy, and a kind of "neurology of humor" niche area of study that is illuminating. What exactly is humor? How does the body produce laughter? What's going on in the brain? We'll dive into all this briefly in the following pages, and my goal is for you to physically feel the benefit of lightheartedness, away from the heavy, serious weight so many of us carry around all the time.

Your Aliveness Salience

In chapter 5, we learned about mortality salience, how aware and sensitive an individual is to their own mortality and the inevitability of death, as well as my iteration of it, aliveness salience, which is being awake to one's own life and individuality. Part of the idea is coming face-to-face with reality, yes. But just as important is to look at everything in front of you, acknowledge the truth of it all, and maintain the ability to laugh about it.

Humor and comedy elicit joy, thereby potentially increasing one's aliveness salience—an alertness to fun, humor, and the thrill of being alive, including one's own thoughts and perspective on life and the world. Whereas researchers are studying the use of virtual reality to gauge people's mortality salience, comedy in the twenty-first century is, in a tangible way, a form of aliveness salience because it gauges comfort level with a wide range of emotions, including slight offense, as well as cathartic relief, connection to storytelling and the emotions of others, and the very real sense of feeling alive alongside other people in a room or theater.

In other words, comedy is vital. It breeds vitality and aliveness. That said, it's crucial to understand the ways in which individuals and communities today struggle to "take a joke." We want to understand the ways in which humor is enormously helpful and healthy for human beings, and for our wider culture and society.

Humor, from a neurological perspective, is thought to occur as a mechanism to reinforce social bonding and to allow disagreeable feelings to surface in a more acceptable way. Humor is also thought to release pent-up stress and tension, serving a physiological function. Other theories suggest that humor plays a role in mate selection, as an indicator of "fitness." It's not hard to imagine that laughing together would help a tribe feel closer, reinforcing shared experiences as members reflect on the day, or that the release of nervousness through laughter would also help uncomfortable topics land a little easier as opposed to in a very serious conversation where stakes are high and tempers are on alert. When laughing, people are more at ease, and being able to finesse one's way through social settings and tense situations certainly makes one more appealing as a potential partner.

The pathway of what comes to be known as "funny" is the simultaneous occurrence of two incongruous or perpetually unexpected phenomena—that is, as Boston College researcher Jessica Black and her colleagues suggest in *Nature Reviews Neuroscience*, "an unexpected violation of expectations, convention, fact or intention," which "results in cognitive arousal; and incongruity resolution associated with amusement." This is known as the incongruity detection and resolution theory. In sum, they write, "Humour helps us to communicate ideas, attract partners, boost mood and cope in times of trauma and stress. These beneficial manifestations are complemented at the physiological level, with humour acting as a natural stress antagonist that can potentially enhance the cardiovascular, immune and endocrine systems." For our purposes, it might also be the case that the clash of *ideas* produces a fertile environment for excitement and laughter, further making the case that healthy friction is not only acceptable but also endearing and attractive.

What Black and her colleagues write about is fascinating. They explore the concept of *Duchenne laughter*, a term coined to capture a basic free-play expression of smile and humor resulting from not only the resolution of incongruous events, but also tickling, for example. "Duchenne laughter is primarily elicited in situations in which a sudden unexpected change in events occurs within a safe social surrounding," they write. There also appears to be a connection between the sensation of being tickled and the kind of free laughter exhibited by kids and adults. Darwin even called humor the "tickling of the mind." And indeed, the excitement that many feel at the spontaneous counter of an idea might be akin to the tickling of the mind, which would explain the soaring popularity of independent media that features diverse and dissident thinkers on podcasts, YouTube, and elsewhere.

According to researchers Joseph Polimeni and Jeffrey Reiss, "The ability to generate and perceive humor is a biological process—a cognitive phenotypic trait—almost certainly dependent on a corresponding genetically based neurological substrate." They continue to say that humor is evolutionarily adaptive. "To our knowledge, no culture exists that is unfamiliar with humor. It appears that all healthy individuals reliably comprehend obvious attempts at humor." In fact, some of the happiest countries, where smiling and laughing are rated by its citizens as occurring the most frequently, are also countries that contain some of the most rural villages, as well as high levels of poverty, like Paraguay and Guatemala, according to recent Gallup World Polls. Polimeni and Reiss say that laughter is, in many ways, a biological reflex, just as the cornea of the eye produces the blinking reflex when stimulated. Humor helps promote bonding, reduces stress during tense situations, and generally reinforces positive social interactions via the pleasant experience of laughter. Humor is also central to courtship, and in some cases has even been found to boost immunity. That is, laughter produces endorphins, reduces cortisol, releases anti-infective antibodies, and reduces blood pressure.

So, to begin to thwart something as evolutionarily adaptive and healthy as humor into a hypervigilant state of fear is actually a dangerous phenomenon, robbing human beings of a biologically wired human impulse that helps in the management and functioning of the everyday life of the individual. Restraining comedy also robs communities and society as they work together to live alongside one another. Comedy is a kind of secret sauce or magic potion, and yet we've so twisted its role in our society that people are now poisoned without its presence.

When People Are Offended Too Easily

A 2022 article in the *Los Angeles Times* written by Sonaiya Kelley proclaims at the top of the piece, "For as long as people have been able to publicly voice their dissent, some version of cancel culture has existed." She discusses rampant hostility online and endless scrolling and writes, "Nowadays, cancel or outrage culture can be a social addiction in itself." And she quotes comedian Tiffany Haddish, who said, "I really believe that the comedian, over the course of history, has been the needle-mover, the one to point out the downfalls and faults in society and everybody doesn't necessarily like that."

Between 1946 and 1981, stand-up comedians were occasionally arrested for "obscenity charges," upheld by the law. Comedian Marty Wayne spent six months in prison in 1946 and the venue operators were charged fees as well. Newsletters wouldn't print what the exact obscene statements were, wanting to avoid duplicating the obscenity, but comedy historian Kliph Nesteroff notes that it was probably "pretty mild." In the early '60s, comedian Lenny Bruce was arrested five times on obscenity charges in San Francisco, LA, Chicago, and New York, with undercover cops and district attorney judges showing up to document his statements on stage. By the early 1970s, obscenity laws had mostly faded, but comedian Richard Pryor was arrested in 1974 for violating a "foul language" rule. His crime? He used a swear word on stage, and the cops cited "disorderly conduct" since obscenity laws no longer stood. Racism likely played a role as well. Then in 1981, comedians John Bowley and John Wilson faced up to a year in prison for talking about "farts" during a show, when a parent of a sixteen-year-old called local authorities to complain.

One example of where strategic challenging of social norms through comedy ultimately *did* go well, despite initial backlash, was the 1970s show *All in the Family*. The show featured a working-class family and confronted many taboo topics of the time, including race, class, and gender, and pushed national conversations forward, both off-screen and on future shows. *All in the Family* is widely credited as having paved the way for shows such as *The Jeffersons* and *Good Times*. What's especially notable is the collaboration that happened behind the scenes to get *All in the Family* on the air; as *The Atlantic* reports, "That *All in the Family* not only reached the air but prospered was the result of two men: Norman Lear, its staunchly liberal creator, and Robert D. Wood, the conservative president of CBS, who put it on the schedule."

These days, there are well-known controversies surrounding comedians like Dave Chappelle, resulting in mass protests at Netflix headquarters and online, and then there are other instances of less-famous comedians actually being completely canceled, losing contracts, and disappearing from active public life. In Chappelle's case, he has a history of making jokes about marginalized communities. While some people feel he goes too far, Netflix has decided to keep his contract and continues to air new stand-up specials by him.

News coverage of comedians facing cancelation tends to only focus on large stars who are canceled for overt remarks, not the subtle jokes that require more in-depth critical thinking and that, when looked at more closely, might not reveal overt hate or racism. One of comedy's most widely acknowledged "least controversial" comedians, Tom Papa, has said, "There are real people that are running into real problems and people that have no ill will being called out. That is a very real thing, and it's not even just the big stories, it's smaller stories that you don't even hear about." Despite his own reputation for being "safe," even he had a game show hosting gig canceled when someone discovered an old joke of his they didn't like from ten years prior.

Spreading genuine hate under the guise of "comedy" is reproachable. But catering to the most sensitive or most extreme individuals is not an advisable strategy either. In *The Journal of Aesthetics and Art Criticism*, Phillip Deen writes, "While they have a claim to set the ideal level of moral sensitivity, it is not an absolute one. . . . An audience is ill-suited to make aesthetic and moral judgments about jokes when their moral offense prevents them from appreciating the joke as a joke." He continues, "Without scrutiny, funniness and the moral rightness of telling jokes is defined by the most sensitive person in the room, and it is rarely a good idea to allow the extreme to set the standard for everyone." Catering to an outlier complaint would strip the joy of entertainment to a flat form of art. Everyone has the right to choose to attend a show, or leave a show, and accept the risk of being offended. Freedom of expression and, in some ways more important, access to joy and communal bonding through laughter are too valuable to give up.

At some point, we all need to ask ourselves if we can simply accept that some comedy will offend us, and that that offense doesn't always mean harm. If I feel offended, it doesn't mean that a show should be canceled. Likewise, we need to resurrect an appreciation of the historical role that comedy has played in illuminating social ills, whether we like what we're hearing or not. It's rare that we let a singular talented storyteller take the stage and push the envelope for millions of viewers to behold. The question of where to draw the line between pushing the envelope and crossing boundaries will always be up for debate and is part of the beauty and dance of democracy and freedom of expression. But when the public is so swayed by emotion and not critical thought, it's a lot harder to tell what we actually believe.

Saying the Quiet Part Out Loud

The fact is that we are all operating in charged environments. Sometimes, it feels like tension is everywhere, even in our own homes or in our friendships. People are stressed, and research has shown that political polarization tends to make people more sensitive overall. Studies have also documented that "humor perception" is lower in individuals with depression and anxiety. I've thought about this at length and wonder what came first.

Are we a depressed society due to polarization and therefore find fewer things funny, or has self-silencing and the suppression of free expression made us more polarized? Polarization, self-silencing, and lower humor perception all swirl together to create more loneliness, isolation, and disconnection, making it difficult to pinpoint how we collectively got ourselves to a place where we're afraid to make jokes and connect through laughter.

Some humor or behavior crosses the line, and some doesn't, depending on who's watching—and at some point it's important to acknowledge that not everything is for everyone. This feels obvious to say out loud, that there is natural human diversity in sensitivity levels, and what each person finds funny or offensive differs. But laughter is a stress reliever and should be viewed as such. If we imagine it like medicine, can we really let ourselves be offended by it? If you're staring at your cold medicine or fitness supplements, can you really be mad at them? If we approach humor in this way, perhaps we can be more forgiving, thereby leveraging the medicinal effects of comedy, laughter, and humor, which include reducing stress and helping us feel closer to others. Feeling close to others also improves overall mood and well-being, so comedy, laughter, and humor truly are potent medicines for our bodies and minds.

In everyday situations, I like to imagine every individual as their own little planet, with their own distinct topography and solar system, and each person's world is inside of a giant beach ball—you know, those large, light, bouncy, airy balls from when we were kids. I imagine the spaciousness around each person, inside the beach ball, and imagine the vibrant world they inhabit, distinct from the next person across from them. I marvel at their world and how different it is from mine, and I peer at them with fascination, as though I'm staring out into a display or exhibit, and I'm ready to learn. As a journalist, especially as a writer interested in psychology, I walk around fascinated by every human I come across.

With that fascination, with that delight, I am also able to smile and laugh a little bit more. I leverage the fascination and delight to help me power through uncomfortable viewpoints that I disagree with, and I approach such interactions as though I'm reading or learning about something I had never even heard of. Again, how fascinating! I take in what I'm hearing and integrate it into my own world as another viewpoint that exists out there in the universe, and I feel like I'm adding to my own knowledge database just by encountering someone so different from me. We can all find humor and happiness in the process of exploration, delighting in new discoveries.

Laughter Therapy

Mary Teegarden is a therapist in California who focuses on not only the potential of laughter in improving mood, but also the role of nature, and she seemed the perfect person to turn to with big philosophical and psychological questions about how people might find a way out of the loneliness and isolation of our virtual algorithmic existence.

She specializes in working with people who describe themselves as sensitive and who take on a lot of the weight of the world and the pain and heaviness of modernity. She is sharp and sensitive herself, a deep thinker who synthesizes all aspects of well-being to work with high-impact, successful people.

One day, she went to a local workshop about laughter yoga and felt there was something to this practice of forced laughter, which sounds like an oxymoron. She realized that laughter is innate, and it is also free. "Adults are so serious and forget how to play, which is not good for overall well-being. So, I decided to start laughing on my way to work. And the premise of laughter yoga is you don't need jokes—the founders had done research on laughter in medicine and gathered people in parks to tell jokes." But, she says, over time the humor being shared in the park turned too offensive, and it wasn't making people laugh as much. At that point they explored forced laughter and found the body still responded positively.

I point out to Teegarden that one of the common threads I hear as she describes her life's work is the role of physicality—that is, laughter, yoga, and being in nature with horses, and she also tells me that she's an avid runner. "People are so removed from their physical selves," I tell her.

She says that the COVID-19 pandemic drove many people outdoors and into their bodies. "Pain thrives in disconnection—from self, the natural world, and each other. We are very disconnected, and technology is a big part of that. People are suffering, living isolated lives," she tells me. But she shares that her clients find a sense of home and connection once they're off their screens. "I believe in consistency, and in having actions that you take," she says, referring to daily walks, yoga, and laughter.

I ask her about how self-silencing and cancel culture might be contributing to the psychological health of society. Does she see the effects in her clients? "I don't think we fully know what the impact is yet," she responds. "My recommendation is to be careful."

"People are becoming more pessimistic about the human experience in general," she says. "People are losing hope. A lot of people are in survival mode. It's heartbreaking."

Then I bring up the importance of getting grounded in one's own body. I know things like cooking and hiking are vital to my own sense of groundedness. "Yes," Mary says. "Back to the basics. It's not about more, more, more. That leaves people empty."

I ask if Mary has any guidance or tips. Are there practical takeaways for such big important life questions? "Every day do something that lights you up, no matter how small. Don't put it off. Every day there has to be something that fills you with hope, that makes you glad to be alive, no matter how small. For me it's stargazing. Just the simplest thing. Find what is beautiful. There is so much that is beautiful here, and we have to reconnect," she says. "So, find ways to connect in a way that lights you up." She reiterates the importance of nature, of laughter, and of not letting go of either. "It's not okay to sink and to get mired in pain," which she compares to drowning.

When I ask her if she has any final thoughts to share, she tells me that she feels hope knowing that I and other writers are thinking about these topics and "doing the work." She wants to see more people come home to themselves; nature, laughter, and embodiment are ways to exit the chaos of our virtual lives.

At the heart of my own concern for my profession—for other writers and journalists—is that there is a stifling of expression and a hiding of one's gifts, a silencing due to the fear of speaking up.

"It's the difference between identity and essence," she says. "People need to live in their essence. . . . People get pulled into identity, but that's not necessarily who we really are, the essence of who we are. I recommend living in your essence as much as you can—and that's where childlike play, laughter, and connection to nature can all help. . . . They are connections to yourself."

Perhaps it comes down to taking yourself—and the categories you define yourself with—less seriously. "Identity can change. It should change. These days there's no flexibility, and we're hurting each other as a result," she concludes. "It requires a little bit of humility to let go."

Chapter 10

The Capital of Complex Thinkers

Go out on a limb with me here for a minute: Imagine the internet as a capital city.

Up until now, the internet has remained an amorphous entity where we (virtually) dwell. It exists as a kind of floating limb attached to our brains. But let's reimagine it in a more concrete way: The internet is now a floating city, a physical metropolis we inhabit. Each of us populates it; there are roads and back alleys, high-rises and tunnels, leaders and those at the fringes. There are lush parks, where some choose to gather in groups, and others jog gently by themselves through the parks' rocky paths. Others sit quietly in basement bars cooking up resentment and manifestos about power. Some wave flags in parades down main boulevards.

Now let's draw our attention to the human body. In psychology there is a term, *interoception*, which refers to the ability to name one's internal experience and the links between sensations, emotions, and behaviors. Naming "I am hot" enables a person to then say, "I feel agitated." "I am hungry" enables a person to then say, "I am becoming angry."

The internet has existed as a city all along, but the lack of naming it as such has prevented us from taking the next step to say, "I feel lonely in this place" or "I feel lost here" or "I feel angry about this place." It is so amorphous that while some people might take some pleasure when opening Instagram and absolute displeasure when opening X, it all feels like one overwhelming visit. "I hate this city," one might say, while still returning to visit again and again.

Naming it as a city—and not just any city, but the ruling capital city, because of how this place influences all other sites of mass media, including film and television—also takes the sting and confusion out of our interactions with it. Many people feel lost, lonely, alienated, and isolated—*and now we know why.*

To continue with this metaphor, let's all think of ourselves as city planners. If you had the opportunity to help build a city, why would you choose to walk down streets that had already been developed by liars and vengeful people and then complain about how those streets made you feel, when you could simply walk across the road and start developing your own neighborhood in a positive, intentional way? In our virtual capital, you have the precious opportunity to engage your whole self, with all your interests and talents, in the creation of meaningful interactions and person-to-person relationship building in a new little universe.

In the meantime, however, we're all in this weird, loud, crowded giant online city that is spilling over into our offline lives. How do we build anew? Where do we go from here, especially regarding the entrenched identities and avatars that have taken hold of the internet's residents?

When we think of the internet as a "capital city" and think of ourselves as designers, we can become more intentional about laying the communications groundwork for how we want that city to function.

In our current world, there is a level of depth that complex thinkers long for when in the company of others, but there have not been many acceptable places for complex thinkers to dwell. Many become writers, researchers, professors, and psychologists, but even in typical academic institutions or literary circles it feels as though depth and nuance are being squeezed out, save for some niche Substacks or podcasts. There is almost an ache when I speak with complex thinkers, as though they're not sure how far to tread, how deep to go. While this restraint is useful at times, it's dangerous for it to become an overall trend. It is also painful to observe.

As we build our new internet city, steering interactions toward grounded, critical, complex thinking is an essential step away from the overcrowded conformist centers that have been eroding the heart of our city. So one thing is clear: We have to make complex thinkers feel more at home in order to one day achieve the dream of having a city of thriving, authentic, dissenting individuals.

Carving Out Space for Complexity

When working toward a more complexity-friendly global community that serves a wildly diverse population of differing viewpoints and backgrounds, the goal is to think through how to empower everyone to feel safe to question and express themselves and create environments in which challenges aren't seen as threats—that is, where disagreement can not only be communicated respectfully but also be seen as a sign of respect. In other words, "safe" in our new world might mean "safe to challenge." For example, I don't feel safe when everyone agrees with me; I feel safe when I know that people are empowered to think for themselves and that their resulting actions, decisions, and behaviors are based in authenticity. Genuineness in communication and interactions makes me feel safe because I am reassured that whatever thoughts, impressions, and conclusions I am forming in response to another person are based on reality and not on false projections.

Regarding our actual offline world today, I see high intelligence and rationality on all political sides, but a sense of primal tribal belonging often takes precedence over critical reasoning.

In other words, it has become too easy to create lavish arguments for a particular stance purely based on tribal belonging, as opposed to critical thought. So how do we move away from the tendency toward tribalism or extremism and model what might be expected in a society built around embracing nuance and complexity? In chapter 7 on speech and debate, the coaches alluded to how their students gain in-depth exposure and immersion into how refined thinking and argument pave the way for respect and new insights. There is no room for extremism, because to be an extremist would be to embrace intense emotion and forgo the useful skill of seeing all perspectives. In short, we need to spread this culture of debate exposure into wider civil society and to the world of the internet.

As Dutch researchers Alain Van Hiel and Ivan Mervielde write, "The degree to which a given political position is associated with complexity depends on the number of conflicting values a person with that position must engage when thinking about a given issue." They continue, "High complexity indicates that a decision-maker carefully weighs all the relevant perspectives on an issue and then integrates them into a coherent position. Low complexity, in contrast, indicates that only one viewpoint is considered, which is maintained with dogmatic tenacity."

It is the dogmatic tenacity so often exemplified on social media and news networks that is corrosive for the toleration of diverse viewpoints. To loosen the grip of dogmatism and extremism means to pivot toward humility and vulnerability—that is, to maintain a kind of openness. It is also helpful to remember the beach ball analogy from the previous chapter, that every person is walking around inside their own little universe. One beach ball doesn't threaten the other—they can bounce off each other. In this new city, we can hold space for complexity and conflict while interacting with others with curiosity and delight. We can embrace the joy of dissent while maintaining respect for disagreement.

Civil Discourse

One of the most formative influences for modeling tolerance and respect in any society is our educational system. How do we build a new city that embraces the healthy debate we read about in chapter 7? How do we resist the self-silencing culture that has taken over at so many universities? How do we push back on the tendency for offense to be mislabeled as harm?

Andrew Jason Cohen is a philosophy professor at Georgia State University, where he is focused on toleration and civil discourse, but in the past five years he has grown increasingly concerned with practical exercises that professors and students can engage in to revive debate and freethinking.

Cohen includes a statement on all of his syllabi at Georgia State:

> I highly value honest and unimpaired, but respectful (and hopefully friendly), dialogue. You should not pretend to think I am (or anyone else you respect, is) right

> when you don't; I will extend you the same courtesy. To do otherwise, I think, is to fail to show respect. If you don't indicate your disagreement, it would seem that you think your interlocutor is not worth correcting—i.e., that you do not respect her. As I come to the class assuming you are worthy of respect, I will indicate when something you say is questionable, leaves you committed to something I reject, or even that you are simply wrong (but feel free to challenge me!). I expect you to do the same (and I may challenge you!). I expect this sort of respectful behavior of all in the class. It is my hope that this will allow for a maximally tolerant, open, and honest discussion.

Cohen is simultaneously concerned that "harm" from speech is exaggerated and at the same time acknowledges that speech can and does cause some harm. The issue is how much? And to what extent? And what if the harm should theoretically insult an entire group, but the individual members experience its effects to varying degrees? He writes, "The problem is that some think that if a student feels offended—an entirely subjective phenomena—that is enough to warrant interference with a speaker." But, he says, "in the college environment, the real harm is caused when students are not challenged." He continues, "Given that the purpose of college is to have one's views challenged, being challenged—even by truly heinous claims—is extremely unlikely to be wrongful and so unlikely to be harmful. Moreover, small wrongful hurts—i.e., harms—

will count as de minimis and not be interfered with. Shutting down speech to protect one student from a minor harm is too risky. The risk of not challenging countless other students—a great wrong—is too high."

Cohen, who is also newly involved with national advocacy around civil discourse, is refreshingly levelheaded. He does not come across as fiery or extremist, nor passive, but rather logical and grounded, as though he wants people to have better conversations simply because it's irritating when they don't. He's pragmatic, and that makes his writing easy to absorb. In one of his papers, he offers a practical note about students, dorm life, and safe spaces:

> It's not at all unreasonable to want one's home to be a "safe place" where one can get away from intellectual challenge. But a college campus is not a home. Even a college dormitory is not a normal home—or at least should not be. A campus dormitory should be a place where college students live as college students. That is to say, a place where they discuss, debate, learn, and grow. It should not be free of intellectual debate, but should be continuous with the rest of college life. Many of us think we learned as much, if not more, in nonclassroom space at college as we did in classroom space. In any case, it is clear that classrooms are not the only places of learning and growing. Anyone demanding that his entire dorm be a space safe from debate is indicating a desire to not be a college student. That desire can be met only by his

> withdrawal from the college. Of course, we all do want and need some space that is safe for our own contemplation, relaxation, regrouping, etc. For college students, that place is often in their own dorm room. That space is, roughly, their genuine home—and there they are and should be free to block out the outside world in safety. That is the only space where freedom of speech should not be respected on a college campus. Visiting someone's college dorm room is visiting their home. There, they make the rules. Everywhere else on the college campus, though, is subject only to the rules of academic integrity.

Cohen tells me in an interview, "A real college is meant to be a place where you become a well-rounded individual, and that requires that you brush up against people that you disagree with—and that requires that you think through all sorts of ideas, even ideas that you hate."

When I bring up that algorithms seem to reinforce polarization, he shares that "the empirical evidence says we're polarized in that each side thinks that the other side has terrible views and so hates the other side, but we're not actually polarized in having different ideas. There isn't as much disagreement as people think there is. But the two sides think there's a lot of disagreement and they think the other side has terrible views that are evil, even though they don't actually disagree about very much."

I ask him about his observations of his students generally, and he tells me about an exercise where he asks a class of forty students to openly share their views about serious moral and political questions. And he says that while students are hesitant at first to say the wrong thing or to challenge one another, once they see that they can honestly share and challenge each other, "they get really into it." "They enjoy it, and the conversations continue after the class is over. So that's a mainstay for my classes, and I'm always thrilled when my students come back and tell me that these conversations continued after. It's a little surprising to me at a school like Georgia State because there's fifty thousand students here and it's mostly a commuter school, but they are going home and discussing with friends and family, and that's what I want to see. I'm always pleased when I see it happening regularly."

Cohen's takeaway is that people want to have discourse, but they are afraid. He's not surprised, but he wants to change that. To that end, the statement that appears in his syllabus is intentional; he wants students to know upfront that he wants them to challenge him and that he wants to challenge them.

He also advises that people should assume others have reasons for what they believe and value. He thinks there are five underlying reasons behind beliefs—that it's wrong to harm people, it's wrong to harm oneself, it's wrong to offend or shock or be rude, that people should help others, and that people should be moral. He thinks that one of those five underlying reasons is behind most beliefs, and so if people start there, they can ask questions to better understand someone with opposing viewpoints. How is someone experiencing harm from a campus speaker? How significant is the harm? Is it just obnoxious? Will it offend? These are all hypothetical questions he thinks about.

He advises people to really dig into the specific questions.

"Assume they have a reason, guess that it's one of those five, and then try to dig into that." And the effect, he hopes, is that things become less heated as the questions force people to think about what's really bothering them.

I share with Cohen that his tips remind me of my conversations with debate coaches from earlier in this book; there is a similar process of preparing for debates and anticipating what the other side might say, especially judges. And on the topic of young people learning to debate, he has some thoughts as well.

He says, "I think we dissuade children from getting into arguments, in a philosophical sense," he responds. "Children ask tough questions all the time—it's just a matter of curiosity." But when we tell them it's bad to argue or ask tough questions, he says they believe it.

We are asking a lot of individuals, I tell him. So many people are raised in ways that counter the development of critical reasoning. It's possible that those who aren't raised with that barrier, in families where critical thought is encouraged—across all spectrums of demographics—are actually advantaged in ways we don't often talk about. For those who are not taught to question, there will be limits to their own explorations of life. Because we disadvantage so many people in this way—where masses of people aren't learning the tools and skills to engage in discourse—this disadvantage might actually help explain why we are collectively having such a hard time.

As we venture into this new territory and confront the difficulties that come along with it, do not withdraw from life itself. If you desire no debate, no challenge, you are not living. Remind yourself of this when you encounter challenges or are supporting friends or raising children; it is intellectual pushback that allows for growth and the blossoming and sharpening of the mind.

In this new city, we must sow our love of uncertainty, and we must let go of the labels that previously acted as chain-link fences. Instead of fixed identities based on group affiliation, we can open ourselves up to individual, shifting containers. Imagine where permanent walls used to be, we plant seasonal hedges, not meant to last forever but to serve us best in whatever phase we find ourselves in. When they no longer serve us, we can rip them out and plant anew.

Embracing Temporary Identities

During the writing of this book, I experienced a kind of split, where on the one hand I was having the meta-experience of writing about the virtual world—and simultaneously feeling sucked into it—and on the other hand, my family and I had just moved into our dream house in the hills and got our dream dog, and I had so much more abundance in the real world than I had ever had before. Why was I writing about this topic? I started to feel burned out and sought out nature intensively. I would feel amazing when visiting the nearby rivers and beaches, but I'd come home and the same feelings of fear and overwhelm would return.

I started to wonder, "Had I been tricked? Had I been under

the spell of X when all I really needed to do was log off?" I wasn't sure escaping social media long-term was even an option, especially for a person who cares about ideas and engagement and democracy. The reality is that we all need to pay attention to what happens online, and of course from the vantage point of writers and journalists, it's a necessity to document what goes on online. But was the answer to my philosophical angst a simple matter of taking a break and touching grass?

Yes, and no.

On the one hand, yes, I desperately needed to submerge my body in a forest for an extended period. On the other hand, my concerns remained, not so much about politics, but about sharing what I knew deep within about a kind of *freedom* to be found outside the bounds of one's "group" or group identity.

So, I got on my laptop to see if any academics were conceptualizing identity as temporary, in the way I had come to view it, and once again I found myself in good company, with philosophers and psychologists alike exploring the phenomenon.

In "Globalization and the Liminal: Transgression, Identity and the Urban Primitive," Loyola University professor Lauren Langman and writer Katie Cangemi examine the role of cities as sites of the liminal—that is, transitory people with transitory identities not only passing through towns and railroads but also passing through their own temporary phases of life, development, and identity. Langman is a social theorist trained in human development, with numerous publications on human nature in the context of globalization and capitalism. He and Cangemi point to ancient carnivals and other sites where social norms are cast aside in service of new ways of being that are emerging in the world, often in reaction to strict moral codes. It strikes me that what is happening on social media now is exactly the same; fringe identities bloom, and people try on new masks. Rebellion is alive, and at the same time temporary as people pass through certain phases and then move on. In our capital city of the internet, the roads and highways are streams of thought, and tunnels are places where people's ideas and identities transition. Change is a constant moving force, and it is central to what it means to be alive.

Where I think it's vital to stay actively engaged online is in the pushing back against narrow conceptions of humanity—that is, all of us need to continually and accurately represent ourselves as the changing, nuanced creatures that we are. Where we have gotten ourselves into trouble is oversimplifying our complex realities and then falsely believing that others can be reduced to those oversimplifications, in denial of our full humanity. "Identity" is a limited concept, a heuristic that functions as a tease—skin color, religion, sexuality, class, profession, and gender are all snapshots but they are not the whole picture.

Aside from being a site to explore and expand identity, the internet and social media are places where "cool" is workshopped and what is fringe and new and exciting gets tackled with vigor as people from all walks of life come together to sort through what feels interesting and strange and daring as opposed to old and already worn. As Cangemi and Langman write, "Liminal realms are times and sites of freedom. . . . The liminal realm is often the site for resistance struggles, inversions, and repudiations, indeed flouting norms and expressions of acts or feelings that are usually forbidden or taboo."

The liminal is the gray area of being antiestablishment or "punk," where one is countering current modes of power and convention. Clearly, the internet is now home to the outcasts and misfits that once characterized the big city environments like the one I grew up in in San Francisco—but in the context of virtual environments there is a kind of *antihuman* sentiment that is unleashed, pitting individualized preferences against others, rather than embracing the wildness of humanity, as actual artists often do in physical locations, where dance, art, and theater thrive.

It's as though the internet is where people now go to opt out of civilization altogether, and this virtual world has now translated to the physical world for many, especially for young people, and it confronts us all with how to relate to reality itself—as individuals, families, cities, and communities. Inside our complex city, social media is the carnival, where bodies feed off one another through takedowns, mobs, and pile-ons. "The traditional sources of stability in people's lives, community, workplace and even family have been eroded. . . . Thus, to accentuate one's personality, in essence to become extraordinary, allows one to take control of at least part of one's existence and impose stability," Cangemi and Langman write.

Be a Real Punk

Our new global capital city deserves to be a healthy town full of well-rounded individuals who feel free to express complexity. But as we have seen, the modern "punk" influencer activists now want to be at the center. Whereas real offline punk clubs at the outskirts of urban cities used to maintain a comfortable anonymity in industrial torn-down neighborhoods, there is something about the new online punks that is different—they want to be part of corporate America, paid handsomely to speak at companies about their newest fashionable identity. So it begs the question, how punk are they really? Is the facade of their online punk status on social media being used to weaponize outcast status and mask their true desires? Wanting power isn't new, but pushing to be so visible and mainstream is. Is this a total inversion of power, then? What does that say about the artistry and culture born out of being on the outside to begin with?

It's become too easy to claim outsider status, and it has led to the commodification of the outsider and an entire demographic of internet-dwelling residents. Outsider is now the ticket to the center, not the exit. Powerful structures have unleashed—through algorithms, technological platforms, and the sheer force of information available—currents that now have a life of their own. It's difficult but necessary to blame human beings; checkboxes are cozy to stay inside of, virtual worlds are alluring, and the power of group identification leads people to believe they're always saying and doing the right thing. But commodifying outsider status, what once was born of artistry, just leads to a boring, flat city.

What will happen when the new punks finally do get power? Will their rise signal a friendly occasion, carried out with integrity as their stated aspirations and intentions loftily claim across social media, speaking of equality and harmony? Or is all of the outrage and punk behavior merely hiding an intended power grab? I don't claim to know the answer, but the question must be asked. Throughout history, many times the oppressed also become oppressors. This is a reality we must contend with and not be naive, which is why championing individual thought, integrity, and curiosity are vital for our collective future. We must lead our capital city in an embodied way, prioritizing authenticity and the search for truth.

As Finnish professor Anu Koivunen states in *Family in Transition* by Pihla Siim, "Identity is not a truth or essence that can be found, received, given or adopted, but it can be described as lifelong processes of building and disassembling." Indeed, identity experimentation can be destructive. We construct ourselves and then morph, hopefully productively, but not always.

Straddling competing identities within oneself can also be a challenge, as in the case of dual national loyalty. People of mixed heritage within the United States, born here, also speak of having to straddle different cultures and identities and feeling like they exist in a liminal space in between two worlds, with primary identities morphing and changing.

On the subject of identity and community, psychology professor Jane Kroger argues that there are clear differences between identity structure and identity content. Structure implies what holds an identity together (i.e., ties to family or school or other structure). A person closely bonded with their family may hold a strong religious orientation tied to family identity, and that structural support can remain intact even if the content of their beliefs and identity actually change. The person may move to atheist, implying the identity content has changed, but their strong family ties give them meaning, keeping their identity structure intact. In her view, "Identity structures also appear in a developmental sequence, with progressive movement reflecting an increasingly differentiated and more complex mode of organizing identity elements." That is, how someone identifies is often temporary and moves through phases of inception, exploration, resolving, and completion.

This is also what we witness online; as Tohoku Gakuin University professor Javier Salazar writes, "Social identity is expressed in the group's reality as an unstable set of social representations, ideas and collective constructions." He looks at the context of mass multiplayer online games and observes several groupings with codified meanings that tend to occur in such virtual settings, but which I would argue now define most online life, not just gaming. These are: ingroups, with their inclusion codes; and innergroups within larger ingroups; and then there are close others, far others, and radical others. The "others" groupings are of particular interest; close others are allies and friends, far others are "enemies or antagonistic opposites," and the radical other is the creator or developer of the game.

According to a paper by Pihla Siim on immigrants in Finland, "In transnational and multicultural families, identity and belonging are not primarily connected to a certain place; instead, those features are created and maintained increasingly through discourses." The author writes about identity development through "family talk." She writes, "In these identity discourses different stereotypes are used and various strategies can be chosen to cope with the new environment and situation," referring to the process of immigration, specifically. She states that in her interviews with immigrants, they express feeling multiple identities at once, "a bit Finnish, a bit Russian, sometimes partly Estonian or something else" and that "negotiation of self-image does not seem to work through clear binary oppositions but by combining different cultural backgrounds."

I'm left wondering, in our modern era, aren't many of us identity immigrants within our own nations, within our own regional demographics and psychographics? Are our multiple identities not birthing new forms of cross-label belonging? Siim seems to agree, in the context of the many former USSR immigrants to Finland, and writes, "Positioning oneself cannot be achieved through clear binary oppositions but by combining them, thus creating multiform, hybrid identities."

University of Hawaii professor Guobin Yang says, "Social movements are liminal phenomena. They separate participants from preexisting structural constraints and give them the freedom and power to remold themselves and society. For those involved, the total effect is a threshold effect—the experience becomes a dividing line in personal histories with immediate and long-term consequences." Yang captures the freedom found in being what I call an "identity orphan." It is freeing to not be bound by categories; if we want to genuinely engage and connect as human beings, and not as boxes, we all must hold on to complexity. As Yang writes, "Liminality is inherently emancipating. The sense of egalitarianism and communion it creates tends to level out existing social structures."

I like the idea that casting away finite boxes is good not only for our own psychology but also for our democracy. If we can see each other as complex creatures, then our rules, laws, policies, and social norms become modeled around that complexity instead of a false sense of who we are. As Yang says, "A social movement can be conceptualized as a liminal happening in general social processes. . . . The characteristics of the liminal situation—freedom, egalitarianism, communion, and creativity—provide the conditions for personal change. . . . Rarely do they remain the same." As people fight to be seen in their full humanity, everything changes.

Identity Orphans and Beating the Algorithms

Embracing temporary identities over fixed ones is a radical shift for most people to make. However, here we can take notes from those of us who never identified with permanent or perfectly marketed categories to begin with: identity orphans.

Identity orphans roam in a liminal space, patiently gliding, often in the dark, taking delight in rare encounters with other identity orphans. We know each other when we see each other;

there's no special handshake or nod or wink, but a mere few sentences usually does it. Personally, when I encounter another identity orphan, I feel my chest relax, like coming home to a glimmer of being known, a treasured spark. Drifters from the future.

But polarization will always prevail if we stay silent about the ways in which we defy categories—the very same categories that social media and algorithms thrive on—because of the marketing machine that has segmented the entire world's population into emotional boxes meant to stoke outrage.

Algorithms don't know what to do with you if you are mixed race. They don't know what to do with you if you are "autism adjacent" (seemingly autistic but don't have a full-blown diagnosis), as I hear from so many people. Algorithms wither when you refrain from liking angry tweets. Instead, you being your nuanced self means that reality prevails, authenticity prevails, and human connection maintains a fighting chance. As the author Sherry Turkle writes, "You end up isolated if you don't cultivate the capacity for solitude, the ability to be separate, to gather yourself. Solitude is where you find yourself so that you can reach out to other people and form real attachments." It's about taking a beat, a moment, a pause, and getting grounded in your body. Self-censorship and mob culture have robbed people of scanning their own bodies for their own actual opinions.

Put plainly, exaggerating and emphasizing group identity leads to self-silencing. On the one hand we have this idea that liberation through identity will lead to belonging, but after a while that fantasy gives way to self-sacrifice in the form of holding back the articulation of the personal particulars—of nuance. Therefore it's vital to understand the psychological processes that lead to dogmatism, extremism, censorship, and group ideology.

The situation is dire. When you constantly reinforce a group identity narrative that leaves out the uniqueness of individuals, you are contributing to a falsity. You are contributing to a narrative that lacks completeness. It has holes. Reinforced groupthink leads to the continued silence of not only yourself but others as well, as group members often seek to emulate each other.

It seems that group identity should function as temporary memberships and that transitioning out of such identities need not be a painful process if the expectation is temporary to begin with. Are we not nomadic? Do we not roam not only in place but in our thoughts and ideas as well? As we grow and shed, is our sense of self not made anew? Then why would we expect to remain with a single group or ideology for the entirety of our lives? The labels of today are meant to be temporary places of belonging, birthways to a deeper form of liberation where group labels are no longer necessary.

In our grand capital city of the internet, we can don a thousand costumes of identity over our lifetimes without clinging to them or being chained by them. We get to know ourselves in a deeper way when we try things on, assess them, question them, look in the mirror, talk about them, share them with others, and move on. As information streams come our way and this city continues to grow and build and develop, our minds have the opportunity to become sharper and our hearts softer. What a blessing such a resource is that our ancestors would have been so incredibly grateful for even just a hundred years ago. And most important, for every great thinker, philosopher, or artist who has ever dreamed of a place where everyone can belong and democracy can thrive, as we build our capital together, let's not take for granted what this new place can do for us. If we waste it, we throw away dreams of connection and liberation; if we chain ourselves, our capital will not thrive.

We are more than capable of deep love, true vulnerability, and the capacity for connection and solidarity. In not forgetting our real, human, offline selves, we have a greater chance of reaching those heights.

Conclusion

Perhaps social media should have been rolled out as an event—that is, as a short-term worldwide virtual picnic that lasted for ten years, and then closed. Maybe people should have been encouraged to gather in real life afterward and integrate all the new understandings gained from one another, with the idea that everyone would then get back to a shared physical reality after a period of "open enrollment" in social media. After another five to ten years, social media could open back up again, allowing the global community square to come together and chat and share ideas. Then it would close again, giving everyone time to integrate in real life, then open up again later. And so on and so on.

But as of now, it has been open for too long. It has largely outgrown its usefulness, and now people remain stuck, unable to retreat from the internet party and connect back to real-world relationships and ways of being. This is where our efforts can best be focused going forward.

For me, writing this book taught me more about how to live well offline than about media, politics, identity, or culture. I quickly realized that my questions about speaking up, groupthink, self-silencing, and polarization were really speaking to long-standing questions I had held about the human condition: how to be an individual, what it means to live in a body, how to live well with others, how to negotiate between self and other, and the parallels between how two individuals can bulldoze through tension, just as two countries can. There is no perfect boundary or communication formula. It's all a dance that requires agility and thinking on one's feet. There is no perfect division of resources, whether we are talking about friend groups or romantic relationships or two warring countries.

On a granular level, by observing the many champions of viewpoint diversity interviewed for this book, I learned what many of us are not taught—that is, how to be a fearless thinker and communicator *without fear of response.* I had long lived with a desire for a more exacting way to sharply communicate my observations, efficiently and to the point, without fear. Despite being a passionate lifelong student of the world's history of ideas, I simply did not have the kind of real life immersive exposure or training to let my own critical ideas fully emerge. Our modern mob culture did not help. I longed to learn how to let myself clash and dance in the beauty of critical reasoning and dialogue. Many people relate to this yearning but are afraid. I'm grateful I let myself wander through new territory.

On my own journey toward a freethinking mindset and way of life it was helpful to see clusters of people promoting viewpoint diversity online, and that helped me open up to sharing my own views more freely. If I hadn't at least seen some movement out there, powered by groups of thoughtful individuals, I'm not sure I would have had the courage to shatter what had felt like a cage. In that way, groups of people can serve a productive role—the numbers of people I observed online who dared to speak openly served as a model for me. Ironically, a group of people helped me escape groupthink.

What I also found, however, is that the kind of grounded, nuanced communication I admired online didn't always carry over into the interpersonal sphere. Sure, when people took time to compose posts, they were gracious and on point. But behind the scenes people were not always the sensitive, thoughtful, gentle souls that their words made them sound like. How much more powerful might critical thinkers become if paired with emotional intelligence as well? This is where the many quiet, sensitive, humble souls I've interacted with throughout my career will shine, because there is a strong emphasis on integrity, which includes loyalty—that is, a loyalty to *consistently* practicing one's values across all contexts, from the private to the interpersonal to the virtual. While some people get caught up in the attention and "ego" of winning arguments, there are many humble souls out there who prize logic, fairness, and insight out of a deep reverence for the human mind, not out of wanting attention. In fact, many people don't want attention but care so much about rules, logic, and consistency that getting to the heart and truth of a matter is of the utmost importance to them and their core values. I hope we can amplify their voices and hold them up as guides through the uncharted territory we attempt to navigate in the future.

Moving Forward

As we face an uncertain future, and as paths before us can either lead to more polarization or an increased understanding of one another, we must take to heart our core values and practice them consistently.

Diversity has been an increasingly powerful and uniting value for many societies in recent years, even if implemented imperfectly. Our current focus on respecting all forms of identity has been much-needed, especially for those who are overshadowed. However, we are in desperate need of *viewpoint diversity*, because we are all individuals and there is much *diversity within diversity*—that is, there is diversity of viewpoints *within* groups of people.

As we increasingly confront viewpoint diversity, the skill of critical reasoning becomes an almost equal value, because it is an absolute necessity as we wade through a sea of opinions and champion one another as fellow swimmers. If groups of people hold on to each other while swimming, they inadvertently dunk one another, weighing each other down, and in some cases force others to drown. Critical thinking helps us swim as individuals and stay afloat.

Critical reasoning is a high-demand skill for the coming decades. As we saw in learning about debate clubs, those classrooms are sites of practice for the skills we need for our future. And as models for our future, it's time to pluck those ecosystems out of tiny classrooms and make them the center of our villages, the center of our new global capital. Now is the time for a more concentrated effort toward nuanced critical thinking, and we need extensive training across multiple spheres of life to achieve it, from our schools, universities, and workplaces to our parenting approaches and family life at home.

Thinking critically is not easy, and that is the hard medicine we all need to swallow. One has to be constantly on guard, at least initially as one's skills are developing. If you want to engage in public issues and be thoughtful and informed, your antenna have to remain up. In some ways it is a hypervigilant state, which directly counters what most therapies would teach, which is why it's *also* important to find your own sense of groundedness and balance amid your pursuit of a truly authentic life. You must identify what your goals are as a thinking human being, find professional and personal outlets for your own flourishing, and then carefully tend to your well-being to support your journey. You must find rest, respite, and refueling in order to continue to grow and avoid burnout. Otherwise all the thinking, questioning, and defending will drive you mad and turn you into someone else. Don't get sucked in.

I visited Barcelona as I was concluding the writing of this book. Spain has one of the most dynamic histories in Europe because of its strategic location adjacent to the Mediterranean, North Africa, and the Atlantic Ocean. To study its past is a master class in learning about viewpoint diversity, though it is largely the story of conquest and competition. Yet Barcelona is a truly punk city with the master-blacksmith-turned-architect Antoni Gaudí's whimsical architectural creations dotting the landscape, which look more like manifestations of psychedelic trips than creations from the turn-of-the-century era in which he lived and worked. Barcelona is also the capital of Catalonia, a distinct region of Spain rich with pride in their heritage, and many Catalonian patriots are still fighting for independence.

Despite its punk history, there is something very "analog" about Barcelona, a bustling city where yellow taxis still dot its narrow alleys and wide boulevards. Town squares feature bakeries and coffee shops, and people dance and walk their dogs. People smile and invite you to sit down, as was the case when my family and I got locked out of our Airbnb one night, when the admittedly non-analog virtual key shut down due to a power outage. At 1 a.m., after we'd viewed a flamenco show at the Palau de la Música, the front desk man in the lobby of a small hotel invited us to make ourselves at home, charge our phones, and have some water. The next day while out shopping, I tried on a pair of locally made leather shoes and I imagined the craftsman, in the same vein as Gaudí's blacksmith family, working hard on his creation with other craftsmen in his village. I'm not naive, but I felt enveloped in the experience, cradled in a place where bodies still work, with at least fewer imprints of digital screens than I've come to know living in the United States for so long. I can't help but feel that travel is yet another much-needed antidote to our obsession with labels and categories. To travel is to suspend our old attachments, free ourselves, and let our inner world reconfigure while our bodies rest and our senses lead.

When I returned home, I felt the courage to post something from my offline reflection over to my little online world of Instagram. It was a post about something we might all want to consider about our mental health in the face of deep polarization and groupthink. I decided to name an experience I had realized was accurate for me as "intellectual isolation dysphoria," exploring the loneliness of being an open, critical, nuanced thinker in our era right now and how at times the loneliness almost takes on a physical quality, hence the dysphoria. Of course, the label is not necessary, but the words were impactful to help others feel seen. The "likes" started pouring in, with comments abounding about how much this resonated, and in helping others feel seen, I felt seen, too. Alas, social media can still be utilized as a useful tool.

In the future, to avoid such widespread alienation, we need to let go of all the siloed identity affiliations. While group identity has been galvanized as a way to connect, it has backfired. It seems that we have allowed ourselves to find common ground at what I'll call a single focal point of overlapping *intensity*. This is bad and we should work against it. We have allowed, in some cases, a kind of lowest common denominator to unite us. One might also say excessive group identification has been a form of shared trauma bonding.

I question the necessity of new jargon and terminology, but I do think it's useful to have a common reference point for thinking about new ideas, and the image of a central overlapping point of intensity, like a Venn diagram, can be helpful in *naming* where much of our contemporary bonding has taken place. Rather than bonding over *pain*, we can actively begin to shift toward bonding over *shared values*.

With that goal in mind, here are a few tidbits of advice:

Get outside of your bubble. Let others help you in real life. Let yourself rely on others, like my family did late that night in Barcelona.

Approach your day with wonder. Slow down. Delight in every unknown interaction . . . with a stranger, a bird in the park, a dog on the street. . . .

Abandon identity. Allow yourself to feel a loving embrace of what happens when you let go and sit in your own power.

Talk to someone very different from you. The best way to shatter your preconceived stereotypes about other "groups" is to speak to members with opposing views. I guarantee you will see them more as individuals and humans than ever before, especially if you only thought of them through the lens of a monolithic group.

Remember that tribal belonging and group identity may

not be as important as *feelings of connection*, which might paradoxically be with several people from different nonoverlapping groups.

Speak up. Individuals don't know their blind spots. One person wakes up, says something, and that catalyzes a new understanding for someone else, and on and on. It's not that everyone wakes up and thinks the same thing, but through osmosis each individual awakens to their own inner knowing and their own critical thinking. Trust yourself. Believe in yourself. Bet on you, not the group.

The End, or the Beginning

This book has told the story of a new universe that we have unknowingly birthed together—one that, at first, held great promise, but has since begun to crumble, forcing us to decide how to steer ahead.

One thing is clear. While you may find some sense of connection or belonging online, you cannot get your *full* individual sense of self from the algorithms, virtual groups, or social media. Your sense of aliveness must come from some life-giving component of critical thought, embodiment, nature, travel, and the thrilling clash of dialogue.

Every day, choose group human. It's healthy to want to belong. It's natural, and there can be freedom and liberation in interdependence. It's possible to create healthy constraints in our dance between belonging and authentic expression. Thinking of others out of choice is different from self-silencing out of fear. Healthy, life-affirming forms of connection—spawned from critical reasoning—might just be enough to save us.

All of us have the power to break away, stand up for ourselves, and communicate bravely. But it starts with the willingness, patience, and dedication to unearthing our own internal viewpoint in order to successfully play around with it, bring in new questions, challenge ourselves, and arrive at new ways of seeing. From there, we can communicate more openly to engage in that same dance with others and learn about their lens on the world.

It takes courage to hold complexity, and it takes vulnerability to admit you see things differently or that you want to be challenged. Many of us reach a tipping point where our group affiliations feel stale and we begin questioning our understandings, how we see the world, and the viewpoints we may have been previously attached to. Actively seeking out exposure to difference will help catapult you forward. It might feel scary, new, exciting, or uncertain, but growth is ensured. By learning to challenge yourself, you strengthen your muscle for dissent and life's uncertainties. Taking that strength outward, encouraging others to think critically, and finding people who enjoy and value truthful dialogue as much as you do is a gift like no other. To be your genuine self in the company of others who are their genuine selves is the hopeful vision for our future that we should all strive toward, relentlessly and joyously.

Acknowledgments

I'm grateful for the twists and turns of writing a book that challenges readers (and editors), and there are many who witnessed, engaged, and supported me.

I thank Maya Alpert at HarperOne for her steadfastness and for cheering me on, Shannon Welch for steering the book forward during a pivotal time, Aly Mostel for being an early thought partner on how to bring this project to the public, and Hilary Swanson for being such a graceful and sharp editor and joyful friend. It's been an honor to work with you all on two books, and hopefully many more.

I thank my siblings for the provocative conversations along

the way; early on, my brother shared clips of forward-thinking dialogue happening online, and my sisters asked me probing questions.

To the brave individuals I interviewed—I know some of you don't like that word but in today's world standing up against the crowd is indeed brave—thank you for pushing forward.

I have old friends from around the world whose perspectives were refreshing: James in Kathmandu and Bryan in Bangkok; and Natalie, Annie, and James in the Bay Area.

Mom, I've loved watching your own philosophical evolution, and thank you for first telling me about Meghan's show. :)

Dad, you're a fierce rebel and have always been; while I'm sorry the world has not been more kind to you, I believe with all my heart that the frictions sharpened your insights that much more.

My husband has always modeled sharp critical thinking by default; he's an engineer, and we used to argue a lot, and I joke that I wrote this book, in part, to catch up with his reasoning abilities. Thank you, my dear; I love you and our intense conversations. :)

To my daughter, you are already a fierce critical thinker about to surpass Daddy and me—I am so proud of you and who you are, the questions you ask, the way you challenge us, and your strength and your elegance.

Notes

Introduction

1 *outnumber the human population*: Steven MacKenzie, "Inside the Future of Humanity: Svalbard's Global Seed Vault," *The Big Issue*, March 4, 2020, https://www.bigissue.com/news/environment/inside-the-future-of-humanity-svalbards-global-seed-vault.

2 *from the vault and replant them*: Jennifer Duggan, "Inside the 'Doomsday' Vault," *TIME*, June 26, 2017, https://time.com/doomsday-vault.

3 *One day, the director of the library*: Richard Hutton, "'Misinformation' Led to Librarian's Firing, US Organization Says," *Penticton Herald*, March 28, 2024, https://www.pentictonherald.ca/spare_news/article_b2b8ccdb-46ad-5a1a-8221–45a79f1048aa.html.

6 *Self-silencing is strongly correlated with depression*: Sebastian Pintea and Andreea Gatea, "The Relationship Between Self-Silencing and Depression: A Meta-Analysis," *Journal of Social and Clinical Psychology* 40, no. 4 (2021): 333–58.

6 *according to numerous studies*: Gordon L. Flett, Avi Besser, Paul L. Hewitt, and Richard A. Davis, "Perfectionism, Silencing the Self, and Depression," *Personality and Individual Differences* 43, no. 5 (2007): 1211–22.

8 *My first book*: Jenara Nerenberg, *Divergent Mind: Thriving in a World That Wasn't Designed for You* (New York: HarperOne, 2020).

9 *never thought of neurodiversity as being limited to psychology*: Jenara Nerenberg, "Has 'Neurodiversity' Gone Rogue?" *Medium*, December 13, 2021, https://jenara.medium.com/has-neurodiversity-gone-rogue-3feef155d7a6.

Chapter 1: The Origins of Self-Silencing Culture

19 *Emma Camp, who is autistic, published an op-ed in the* New York Times: Emma Camp, "I Came to College Eager to Debate. I Found Self-Censorship Instead," *New York Times*, March 7, 2022, https://www.nytimes.com/2022/03/07/opinion/campus-speech-cancel-culture.html.

21 *sense social inconsistencies, hypocrisies, and inaccuracies*: Lucy Kross Wallace, "From the Community: When Inclusive Language excludes," *The Stanford Daily*, October 20, 2021, https://stanforddaily.com/2021/10/20/from-the-community-when-inclusive-language-excludes.

21 *patterns that don't follow expected rules*: Simon Baron-Cohen, Emma Ashwin, Chris Ashwin, Teresa Tavassoli, and Bhismadev Chakrabarti, "Talent in Autism: Hyper-systemizing, Hyper-attention to Detail and Sensory Hypersensitivity," *Philosophical Transactions of the Royal Society of London. Series B, Biological Sciences* 364, no. 1522 (2009): 1377–83, doi: 10.1098/rstb.2008.0337.

21 *hide parts of themselves to blend in*: Michelle Cleary, Sancia West, Rachel Kornhaber, and Catherine Hungerford, "Autism, Discrimination and Masking: Disrupting a Recipe for Trauma," *Issues in Mental Health Nursing* 44, no. 9 (2023): 799–808, doi: 10.1080/01612840.2023.2239916.

22 *depression and anxiety often result*: Javad Alaghband-rad, Arman Hajikarim-Hamedani, and Mahtab Motamed, "Camouflage

and Masking Behavior in Adult Autism," *Frontiers in Psychiatry* 14 (2023): doi: 10.3389/fpsyt.2023.1108110.

22 *a study out of the Max Planck Institute of Evolutionary Anthropology in Germany*: Daniel B. M. Haun, Yvonne Rekers, and Michael Tomasello, "Children Conform to the Behavior of Peers; Other Great Apes Stick with What They Know," *Psychological Science* 25, no. 12 (2014): 2160–67, doi: 10.1177/0956797614553235.

23 *author Batya Ungar-Sargon*: Batya Ungar-Sargon, *Bad News: How Woke Media Is Undermining Democracy* (New York: Encounter Books, 2021).

24 *TED, for example*: Coleman Hughes, "Why Is TED Scared of Color Blindness?" *The Free Press*, September 26, 2023, https://www.thefp.com/p/coleman-hughes-is-ted-scared-of-color-blindness.

25 *Thankfully, these and other outlets*: "Adam Grant and Chris Anderson Respond to Coleman Hughes," *The Free Press*, September 27, 2023, https://www.thefp.com/p/adam-grant-chris-anderson-respond-coleman-hughes.

25 *"convenient, even entertaining"*: John A. Teske, "Cyberpsychology, Human Relationships, and Our Virtual Interiors," *Zygon: Journal of Religion and Science* 37, no. 3 (2002): 677–700.

27 *"The diffusion of new communication"*: Giuseppe Riva and Carlo Galimberti, *Towards CyberPsychology: Mind, Cognition, and Society in the Internet Age* (Amsterdam: IOS Press, 2001).

28 *"promoting a level of self-censorship"*: Ioana Kocurová-Giurgiu, "Cancel Culture as Perceived and Encouraged in Academia: An Exploration of How Mob Attitudes on Social media Promote Censorship and the End of Open Dialogue," Skoda Auto University, September 2021.

Chapter 2: The Effects of Groupthink

38 *There was a Canadian teacher*: AJ McDougall, "Ex-Toronto Principal Dies by Suicide After Anti-Racism Training Fiasco," *Daily Beast*, July 25, 2023, https://www.thedailybeast.com/ex-toronto-principal-richard-bilkszto-dies-by-suicide-after-alleged-bullying-at-anti-racism-training.

39 *Over in Minnesota at Hamline University*: "PEN America Cites 'Egregious Violation' of Academic Freedom by Hamline University," *PEN America*, December 23, 2022, https://pen.org/press-release/pen-america-cites-egregious-violation-of-academic-freedom-by-hamline-university.

41 *A 2019 study*: Brian C. Patrick, Sarah Stockbridge, Heidi V. Roosa, and Julie S. Edelson, "Self-Silencing in School: Failures in Student Autonomy and Teacher-Student Relatedness," *Social Psychology of Education: An International Journal* 22, no. 4 (2019): 943–67, doi: 10.1007/s11218–019–09511–8.

41 *literature on self-silencing and depression*: Avi Besser, Gordon L. Flett, and Paul L. Hewitt, "Silencing the Self and Personality Vulnerabilities Associated with Depression," in *Silencing the Self Across Cultures: Depression and Gender in the Social World*, eds. Dana C. Jack and Alisha Ali (Oxford University Press, 2010), 285–312, doi: 10.1093/acprof:oso/9780195398090.003.0014.

41 *reports indicate that roughly 50 percent*: Leonard Cassuto, "PhD Attrition: How Much Is Too Much?" *Chronicle of Higher Education*, July 1, 2013, https://www.chronicle.com/article/ph-d-attrition-how-much-is-too-much.

44 *make people more easily offended*: Jeremy B. Bernerth, "You're Offended, I'm Offended! An Empirical Study of the Proclivity to Be Offended and What It Says About Employees' Attitudes and Behaviors," *Journal of Business Research* 116 (2020): 314–23, doi: 10.1016/j.jbusres.2020.05.040.

47 *Wright has published extensively on this concern*: R. George Wright, "Self-Censorship and the Constriction of Thought and Discussion Under Modern Communications Technologies," *Notre Dame Journal of Law, Ethics & Public Policy* 25 (2012).

49 *researchers call "self-concealment"*: Kenneth M. Cramer, Melanie D. Gallant, and Michelle W. Langlois, "Self-Silencing and Depression in Women and Men: Comparative Structural Equation Models," *Personality and Individual Differences* 39, no. 3 (2005): 581–92, doi: 10.1016/j.paid.2005.02.012.

49 *leads to depression via repressed anger*: Valerie E. Whiffen, Meredith L. Foot, and Janice M. Thompson, "Self-Silencing Mediates

the Link Between Marital Conflict and Depression," *Journal of Social and Personal Relationships* 24, no. 6 (2007): 993–1006, doi: 10.1177/0265407507084813.

49 *what's known as rejection sensitivity*: Rainer Romero-Canyas, Kavita S. Reddy, Sylvia Rodriguez, and Geraldine Downey, "After All I Have Done for You: Self-Silencing Accommodations Fuel Women's Post-Rejection Hostility," *Journal of Experimental Social Psychology* 49, no. 4 (2013): 732–40, doi: 10.1016/j.jesp.2013.03.009.

49 *researcher Daniel Bar-Tal writes*: Daniel Bar-Tal, "Self-Censorship as a Socio-Political-Psychological Phenomenon: Conception and Research," *Advances in Political Psychology* 38 (2017), doi: 10.1111/pops.12391.

49 *Multiple studies show*: https://www.apa.org/monitor/2024/01/trends-hope-greater-meaning-life.

50 *brain's reward system*: Jamie Waters, "Constant Craving: How Digital Media Turned Us All into Dopamine Addicts," *The Guardian*, August 22, 2021, https://www.theguardian.com/global/2021/aug/22/how-digital-media-turned-us-all-into-dopamine-addicts-and-what-we-can-do-to-break-the-cycle.

50 *social media and the "dopamine loop"*: Trevor Haynes, "Dopamine, Smartphones & You: A Battle for Your Time," *Harvard Medical School*, May 1, 2021, https://www.scribd.com/document/460458389/Dopamine-Smartphones-You-A-battle-for-your-time-Science-in-the-News-pdf.

Chapter 3: Vulnerability to Extremism

53 *leading group identity researcher*: Michael A. Hogg, "From Uncertainty to Extremism: Social Categorization and Identity Processes," *Current Directions in Psychological Science* 23, no. 5 (2014): 338–42, doi: 10.1177/0963721414540168.

54 *Uncertainty-identity theory is*: Michael A. Hogg, "Self-Uncertainty and Group Identification: Consequences for Social Identity, Group Behavior, Intergroup Relations, and Society," in *Advances in Experimental Social Psychology* 64, ed. Bertram Gawronski (Elsevier Academic Press, 2021), 263–316.

56 *In a 2018 paper*: Arie W. Kruglanski, Jessica R. Fernandez, Adam R. Factor, and Ewa Szumowska, "Cognitive Mechanisms in Violent

Extremism," *Cognition* 188 (2019): 116–23, doi: 10.1016/j.cognition.2018.11.008.

56 *In a chapter appearing in*: Katarzyna Jasko, David Webber, and Arie W. Kruglanski, "Political Extremism," in *Social Psychology: Handbook of Basic Principles*, eds. Paul A. M. Van Lange, E. Tory Higgins, and Arie W. Kruglanski (New York: Guilford Press, 2022), 567–88.

58 *Michael Hogg writes about "entitativity"*: Michael A. Hogg, David K. Sherman, Joel Dierselhuis, Angela T. Maitner, and Graham Moffitt, "Uncertainty, Entitativity, and Group Identification," *Journal of Experimental Social Psychology* 43 (2007): 135–42, doi: 10.1016/j.jesp.2005.12.008.

59 *After a group becomes*: Zachary P. Hohman, "Fearing the Uncertain: A Causal Exploration of Self-Esteem, Self-Uncertainty, and Mortality Salience" CGU Theses & Dissertations, paper 26 (2012), http://scholarship.claremont.edu/cgu_etd/26.

61 *they "inhabit polarized identity silos"*: Michael A. Hogg and Amber M. Gaffney, "Social Identity Dynamics in the Face of Overwhelming Uncertainty," in *The Psychology of Insecurity: Seeking Certainty Where None Can Be Found*, eds. Joseph P. Forgas, William D. Crano, and Klaus Fiedler (New York: Routledge, 2023), 244–63.

63 *Hogg delivers a reframe*: Michael Hogg, "Social Instability and Identity-Uncertainty: Fertile Ground for Extremism," in *Social Psychology and Politics* (New York: Routledge, 2015), 307–19.

65 *According to researcher Anja Dalgaard-Nielsen*: Anja Dalgaard-Nielsen, "Promoting Exit from Violent Extremism: Themes and Approaches," *Studies in Conflict & Terrorism* 36 (2013): 99–115, doi: 10.1080/1057610X.2013.747073.

Chapter 4: The Strength to Dissent

78 *"loss of personal identity"*: E. Marshall Brooks, "The Disenchanted Self: Anthropological Notes on Existential Distress and Ontological Insecurity Among ex-Mormons in Utah," *Culture, Medicine, and Psychiatry* 44 (2020): 193–213, doi: 10.1007/s11013-019-09646-5.

78 *"Many who leave religion in America"*: Jon Fortenbury, "The Health Effects of Leaving Religion," *The Atlantic*, September 28, 2014,

https://www.theatlantic.com/health/archive/2014/09/the-health-effects-of-leaving-religion/379651/#.

79 *There is even a 2010 study:* Christopher P. Scheitle and Amy Adamczyk, "High-Cost Religion, Religious Switching, and Health," *Journal of Health and Social Behavior* 51, no. 3 (2010): 325–42, doi: 10.1177/0022146510378236.

83 *"freedom from religious conformity"*: Heinz Streib, "Leaving Religion: Deconversion," *Current Opinion in Psychology* (2021), doi: 10.1016/j.copsyc.2020.09.007.

84 *"Group members may dissent"*: Jolanda Jetten and Matthew J. Hornsey, "Deviance and Dissent in Groups," *Annual Review of Psychology* 65 (2014): 461–85, doi: 10.1146/annurev-psych-010213–115151.

85 *Stanford professor Benoît Monin*: Benoît Monin and Kieran O'Connor, "Reactions to Defiant Deviants: Deliverance or Defensiveness?" in *Rebels in Groups: Dissent, Deviance, Difference and Defiance*, eds. Jolanda Jetten and Matthew J. Hornsey (New Jersey: Blackwell Publishing, 2011), 259–80, doi: 10.1002/9781444390841.ch14.

86 *Heterodox Academy is an organization*: Tom Bartlett, "How Heterodox Academy Hopes to Change the Campus Conversation," *Chronicle of Higher Education*, January 9, 2023, https://www.chronicle.com/article/how-heterodox-academy-hopes-to-change-the-campus-conversation.

86 *Foundation for Individual Rights and Expression*: Lexi Lonas, "Protecting Free Speech on Campus from Attacks from Both Sides," *The Hill*, March 5, 2024, https://thehill.com/homenews/education/4506449-protecting-free-speech-campus.

87 *Braver Angels is a grassroots organization*: Lois M. Collins, "Why Political Disagreements Are Healthy, Essential for a Strong Nation," *Deseret News*, June 29, 2024, https://www.deseret.com/politics/2024/06/29/braver-angels-carthage-college-polarized-politics.

87 *Podcaster Coleman Hughes*: Coleman Hughes, "Opinion: A Big Problem with How We Talk About Race Today," CNN, February 5, 2024, https://www.cnn.com/2024/02/05/opinions/black-conservative-race-coleman-hughes/index.html.

87 *The speaker Africa Brooke*: Elle Hunt, "Everyone's So Intolerant

Online. Am I Right to Stay Silent?" *The Guardian*, May 22, 2024, https://www.theguardian.com/wellness/article/2024/may/22/cancel-culture-social-media.

87 *Journalist Bari Weiss*: Max Cohen, "*New York Times* Opinion Writer Bari Weiss Resigns, Citing Hostile Culture and Lack of Ideological Diversity," *Politico*, July 14, 2020, https://www.politico.com/news/2020/07/14/new-york-times-bari-weiss-resigns-360730.

88 *Meghan Daum is a well-known essayist*: Isaac Chotiner, " 'There Is a Hunger Out There for More Complicated Discussions,' " *Slate*, September 4, 2018, https://slate.com/news-and-politics/2018/09/meghan-daum-intellectual-dark-web-identity-politics.html.

90 *A fantastic 2023 debate at MIT*: "First-of-Its-Kind Debate on a US Campus of Diversity-Equity-Inclusion Occurs Peacefully at MIT," MIT Free Speech Alliance, April 4, 2023, https://mitfreespeech.org/news_manager.php?page=32785.

90 *A 1996 paper*: Charlan Nemeth and John Rogers, "Dissent and the Search for Information," *British Journal of Social Psychology* 35 (1996): 67–76, doi: 10.1111/j.2044–8309.1996.tb01083.x.

91 *In a 2018 study*: Michael A. Beam, Jeffrey T. Child, Myiah J. Hutchens, and Jay D. Hmielowski, "Context Collapse and Privacy Management: Diversity in Facebook Friends Increases Online News Reading and Sharing," *New Media & Society* 20, no. 7 (2018): 2296–314, doi: 10.1177/1461444817714790.

92 *In a study out of South Korea*: Dongyoung Sohn, "Spiral of Silence in the Social Media Era: A Simulation Approach to the Interplay Between Social Networks and Mass Media," *Communication Research 49* (2022): 139–66, doi: 10.1177/0093650219856510.

93 *coined the term context collusion:* Jenny L. Davis and Nathan Jurgenson, "Context Collapse: Theorizing Context Collusions and Collisions," *Information, Communication & Society* 17, no. 4 (2014): 476–85, doi: 10.1080/1369118X.2014.888458.

94 *In a 2021 study by Qinfeng Zhu and Marko Skoric*: Qinfeng Zhu and Marko M. Skoric, "From Context Collapse to 'Safe Spaces': Selective Avoidance Through Tie Dissolution on Social Media," *Mass Communication and Society* 24, no. 6 (2021).

95 *A paper by psychologist Bert Hodges*: Bert H. Hodges, "Rethink-

ing Conformity and Imitation: Divergence, Convergence, and Social Understanding," *Frontiers in Psychology* 5 (2014), doi: 10.3389/fpsyg.2014.00726.

Chapter 5: The Courage to Stand Alone

97 *as social science research shows*: Marc Novicoff, " 'It's Causing Them to Drop Out of Life': How Phones Warped Gen Z," *Politico*, March 24, 2024, https://www.politico.com/news/magazine/2024/03/24/the-anxious-generation-qa-00147880.

97 *Yeshiva University professor*: Sanjana Gupta, "What Does It Mean to Feel Overwhelmed?," *Verywell Mind*, January 12, 2024, https://www.verywellmind.com/feeling-overwhelmed-symptoms-causes-and-coping-5425548.

99 *A 2024* Family & Law *article*: Lisette Dirksen, Nadia Ismaïli, Elanie Rodermond, Catrien Bijleveld, and Masha Antokolskaia, "Extremist Beliefs and Child Protection," *Family & Law* (2024), doi: 10.5553/FenR/.000065.

99 *In one of her videos*: Marlene Winell, "Religious Indoctrination as a Child," *JourneyFreeOrg*, YouTube, October 6, 2019, https://www.youtube.com/watch?v=0RQEPWw_D2U.

102 *a known phenomenon called mortality salience*: Immo Fritsche, Eva Jonas, and Thomas Fankhaenel, "The Role of Control Motivation in Mortality Salience Effects on Ingroup Support and Defense," *Journal of Personality and Social Psychology* 95 (2008): 524–41.

103 *many theorists discussing the concept of autonomy*: Reuben Ng, Heather Allore, and Becca R. Levy, "Self-Acceptance and Interdependence Promote Longevity: Evidence from a 20-Year Prospective Cohort Study," *International Journal of Environmental Research and Public Health* 17 (2020), doi: 10.3390/ijerph17165980.

103 *According to leading autonomy researcher*: Richard M. Ryan, Edward L. Deci, Wendy S. Grolnick, and Jennifer G. La Guardia, "The Significance of Autonomy and Autonomy Support in Psychological Development and Psychopathology," in *Developmental Psychopathology, volume 1: Theory and Method*, eds. Dante Cicchetti and Donald J. Cohen (New York: John Wiley & Sons, 2006).

108 *Psychologist Valerie Tarico*: Valerie Tarico, "An Excess of Woke

Thinking May Harm Mental Health or Relationships," Valerie Tarico: psychologist and author website, December 15, 2021, https://valerietarico.com/2021/12/15/an-excess-of-woke-thinking-may-harm-mental-health-or-relationships.

112 *which relates to self-presentation*: Erin E. Hollenbaugh, "Self-Presentation in Social Media: Review and Research Opportunities," *Review of Communication Research* 9 (2021): 80–98, doi: 10.12840/ISSN.2255–4165.027.

112 *"The trove of potential online social media data is vast"*: Margeret Hall and Simon Caton, "Am I Who I Say I Am?: Unobtrusive Self-Representation and Personality Recognition on Facebook," *PLOS One* 12, no. 9 (2017), doi: 10.1371/journal.pone.0184417.

112 *"The emergence of social networking sites"*: Soraj Hongladarom, "Personal Identity and the Self in the Online and Offline World," *Minds and Machines* 21 (2011): 533–48, doi: 10.1007/s11023–011–9255-x

113 *Professor Chris Fullwood and colleagues*: Chris Fullwood, Caroline Wesson, Josephine Chen-Wilson, Melanie Keep, Titus Asbury, and Luke Wilsdon, "If the Mask Fits: Psychological Correlates with Online Self-Presentation Experimentation in Adults," *Cyberpsychology, Behavior, and Social Networking* 23, no. 11 (2020): 737–42, doi: 10.1089/cyber.2020.0154.

114 *Researchers in Europe*: Petter Bae Brandtzaeg and María-Ángeles Chaparro-Domínguez, "From Youthful Experimentation to Professional Identity: Understanding Identity Transitions in Social Media," *YOUNG* 28, no. 2 (2020): 157–74, doi: 10.1177/1103308819834386.

116 *In a joint paper*: Ben Marder, David Houghton, Adam Joinson, Avi Shankar, and Eleanor Bull, "Understanding the Psychological Process of Avoidance-Based Self-Regulation on Facebook," *Cyberpsychology, Behavior, and Social Networking* 19, no. 5 (2016): 321–27, doi: 10.1089/cyber.2015.0564.

119 *"In Japan, the controversy"*: David McElhinney, "Japan Shrugs as Americans Fume Over Gwen Stefani 'Appropriation,'" *Al Jazeera*, January 15, 2023, https://www.aljazeera.com/economy/2023/1/15/japan-shrugs-as-us-fumes-over-gwen-stefani-appropriation-furore.

Chapter 6: Staying True to Ourselves

124 *Brené Brown, for example*: Brené Brown, "The Power of Vulnerability," *TED*, June 2010, https://www.ted.com/talks/brene_brown_the_power_of_vulnerability?subtitle=en.

125 *"Vulnerability without boundaries is not vulnerability"*: Brené Brown, "Brene Brown: The Courage to Be Vulnerable," *Insights at the Edge* podcast interview, https://resources.soundstrue.com/transcript/brene-brown-the-courage-to-be-vulnerable.

128 *A* Chicago Tribune *article by Nick Haslam*: Nick Haslam, "The Problem with Describing Every Misfortune as 'Trauma,'" *Chicago Tribune*, August 15, 2016, https://www.chicagotribune.com/2016/08/15/the-problem-with-describing-every-misfortune-as-trauma.

128 *quoted in a* Metro *article*: Jessica Lindsay, "The Problem with Mental Health Influencers," *Metro*, May 9 2021, https://metro.co.uk/2021/05/09/mental-health-influencers-providing-vital-support-or-hoodwinking-the-vulnerable-14381681.

130 *A former Evangelical Christian*: Valerie Tarico, *Trusting Doubt: A Former Evangelical Looks at Old Beliefs in a New Light* (Virginia: Oracle Institute, 2010).

132 *Tarico suggests a few helpful reframes for individuals*: Valerie Tarico, "An Excess of Woke Thinking May Harm Mental Health or Relationships," Valerie Tarico: psychologist and author website, December 15, 2021, https://valerietarico.com/2021/12/15/an-excess-of-woke-thinking-may-harm-mental-health-or-relationships.

134 *esteemed Columbia University linguist John McWhorter*: Zaid Jilani, "John McWhorter Argues That Antiracism Has Become a Religion of the Left," *New York Times*, October 26, 2021, https://www.nytimes.com/2021/10/26/books/review/john-mcwhorter-woke-racism.html.

135 *"These patterns not only trap"*: Valerie Tarico, "An Excess of Woke Thinking."

135 *Research on complexity, creativity, and high intelligence*: Francis Heylighen, "Gifted People and Their Problems," Free University of Brussels, http://pespmc1.vub.ac.be/Papers/GiftedProblems.pdf.

136 *normal for such "gifted" thinkers*: Francis Heylighen, "Gifted People and Their Problems," Free University of Brussels, http://pespmc1.vub.ac.be/Papers/GiftedProblems.pdf.

136 *psychologist Mary-Elaine Jacobsen:* Mary-Elaine Jacobsen, *Liberating Everyday Genius* (New York: Ballantine Books, 1999).

137 *Psychologist and author Deirdre Lovecky*: Deirdre V. Lovecky, "Can You Hear the Flowers Singing?: Issues for Gifted Adults," *Journal of Counseling and Development* 64, no. 9 (1986): 590–92.

Chapter 7: Debate as the Antidote

143 *Mellessa Denny is an award-winning*: Mike Smith, "Amarillo Teacher Wins Statewide Scholastic Honor," *Panhandle PBS*, January 16, 2018, https://www.panhandlepbs.org/blogs/learn-here/amarillo-teacher-wins-statewide-scholastic-honor.

151 *Studies have shown:* Ruth Kennedy, "In-Class Debates: Fertile Ground for Active Learning and the Cultivation of Critical Thinking and Oral Communication Skills," *International Journal of Teaching and Learning in Higher Education* 19, no. 2 (2007): 183–90.

151 *Contrary to what many believe*: Beth E. Schueler and Katherine E. Larned, "Interscholastic Policy Debate Promotes Critical Thinking and College-Going: Evidence from Boston Public Schools," *Educational Evaluation and Policy Analysis*, doi: 10.3102/01623737231200234.

152 *"in fact, the structure and facilitation of debate"*: AnnMarie Baines, Diana Medina, and Caitlin Healy, *Amplify Student Voices: Equitable Practices to Build Confidence in the Classroom* (ASCD, 2023).

152 *Deanna Kuhn is a leading scholar of critical thinking*: Deanna Kuhn, Laura Hemberger, and Valerie Khait, *Argue with Me: Argument as a Path to Developing Students' Thinking and Writing* (Wessex, 2013).

153 *"It is in argument"*: Deanna Kuhn, "Thinking as Argument," *Harvard Educational Review* 62, no. 2 (1992): 155–78, doi: 10.17763/haer.62.2.9r424r0113t670l1.

153 *"Thinking as argument"*: Deanna Kuhn, "Science as Argument: Implications for Teaching and Learning Scientific Thinking," *Science Education* 77, no. 3 (1993): 319–37, doi: 10.1002/sce.3730770306.

153 *"An average of only 26 percent"*:Deanna Kuhn, "Thinking as Argument," in *Critical Readings on Piaget, ed. Leslie Smith* (New York: Routledge, 1996).

157 *"While most professors have honed"*: Lisa Tsui, "Cultivating Critical

Thinking: Insights from an Elite Liberal Arts College," *The Journal of General Education* 56 (2008): 200–27.

158 *Discussion seems to be especially effective*: Laura C. Edwards, "The Craft of Infusing Critical Thinking Skills: A Mixed-Method Research on Implementation and Student Outcome," *Journal on Centers for Teaching and Learning* 9 (2017): 47–72.

159 *In a 2020 report*: Daniel Muijs and Christian Bokhove, "Metacognition and Self-Regulation: Evidence Review" (London: Education Endowment Foundation, 2020).

164 *"a relatively unnatural, higher order skill"*: John Daniel Cazier, "Fostering Critical Thinking," United States Military Academy, West Point (2010), https://www.westpoint.edu/sites/default/files/inline-images/centers_research/center_for_teching_excellence/PDFs/mtp_project_papers/Cazier_10.pdf.

164 *author of the viral*: Emma Camp, "I Came to College Eager to Debate. I Found Self-Censorship Instead," *New York Times*, March 7, 2022, https://www.nytimes.com/2022/03/07/opinion/campus-speech-cancel-culture.html.

168 UnHerd: UnHerd, https://unherd.com.

168 Compact: Compact, https://www.compactmag.com.

169 *Sarah Haider*: Sarah Haider, *Hold That Thought*, https://newsletter.sarahhaider.com.

169 *Erec Smith*: Erec Smith et al., *Journal of Free Black Thought*, https://freeblackthought.substack.com.

169 *Sheena Mason*: Sheena Michele Mason, *Togetherness Wayfinder*, https://togethernesswayfinder.substack.com.

Chapter 8: Embracing Our Depth

173 *"We let people hold onto"*: Sebastien Bishop and Robert Mark Simpson, "Disagreement and Free Speech," in *Routledge Handbook of Philosophy of Disagreement*, eds. Maria Baghramian, J. Adama Carter, and Rach Cosker-Rowland (New York: Routledge, 2023).

174 *"In a free and democratic society"*: Kathleen McGarvey Hidy, "The Speech Gods: Freedom of Speech, Censorship, and Cancel Culture in the Age of Social Media," *Washburn Law Journal* 61 (2021).

175 *their joint statement*: Robert P. George and Cornel West, "Truth

Seeking, Democracy, and Freedom of Thought and Expression," James Madison Program in American Ideals and Institutions, Princeton University, March 14, 2017, https://jmp.princeton.edu/news/2017/sign-statement-truth-seeking-democracy-and-freedom-thought-and-expression-statement.

178 *In another collaborative media piece*: Patrick J. Deneen, Francis Fukuyama, Deirdre Nansen McCloskey, and Cornel West, "Is Liberalism Worth Saving?," *Harper's Magazine*, October 19, 2022, https://harpers.org/archive/2023/02/is-liberalism-worth-saving-francis-fukuyama-cornel-west-deirdre-mccloskey-patrick-deneen.

179 *In a study of almost five thousand high schoolers*: Siwei Cheng and Yu Xie, "Structural Effect of Size on Interracial Friendship," *Proceedings of the National Academy of Sciences of the United States of America* 110, no. 18 (2013): 7165–69, doi: 10.1073/pnas.1303748110.

179 *According to researchers Young Kim et al.*: Young K. Kim, Julie J. Park, and Katie K. Koo, "Testing Self-Segregation: Multiple-Group Structural Modeling of College Students' Interracial Friendship by Race," *Research in Higher Education* 56, (2015): 57–77, doi: 10.1007/s11162–014–9337–8.

180 *According to research appearing in the* Journal of Social Issues: Elizabeth Page-Gould, Rodolfo Mendoza-Denton, and Wendy Berry Mendes, "Stress and Coping in Interracial Contexts: The Influence of Race-Based Rejection Sensitivity and Cross-Group Friendship in Daily Experiences of Health," *Journal of Social Issues* 70, no. 2 (2014): 256–78, doi: 10.1111/josi.12059.

183 *In this particular case, studies show*: https://www.apa.org/monitor/2024/01/trends-hope-greater-meaning-life.

185 *Psychologist Kathy McMahon*: Kathy McMahon, "The Survival Mindset," *Resilience*, March 15, 2010, https://www.resilience.org/stories/2010–03–15/survival-mindset.

187 *Her steps of religious recovery*: Marlene Winell, "Seven Steps to Recovery," *Debunking Christianity*, February 15, 2009, https://www.debunking-christianity.com/2009/02/seven-steps-to-recovery.html.

187 *Writer Kyle Howington describes GUI*: Kyle Howington, "Survival Psychology and Creating a Survivalist Mindset," The Survival Uni-

versity, https://thesurvivaluniversity.com/survival-tips/understanding-survival-psychology-to-create-a-strong-survivalist-mindset.

188 *centered around "tech sabbaths"*: Emily McFarlan Miller, "The Science of Sabbath: How People Are Rediscovering Rest—and Claiming Its Benefits," *Religion News Service*, September 25, 2019, https://religionnews.com/2019/09/25/the-science-of-sabbath-how-people-are-rediscovering-rest-and-claiming-its-benefits.

188 *Global Day of Unplugging*: GMA Team, "DIY Projects and Games to Enjoy on Global Day of Unplugging," *Good Morning America*, March 1, 2024, https://www.goodmorningamerica.com/shop/story/diy-projects-games-enjoy-global-day-unplugging-107682789.

189 *Researchers on forgiveness*: Kendra Cherry, "How to Forgive Yourself," *Verywell Mind*, December 5, 2023, https://www.verywellmind.com/how-to-forgive-yourself-4583819.

Chapter 9: The Power of Comedy

194 *studying the use of virtual reality*: Luca Chittaro, Riccardo Sioni, Cristiano Crescentini, and Franco Fabbro, "Mortality Salience in Virtual Reality Experiences and Its Effects on Users' Attitudes Towards Risk," *International Journal of Human-Computer Studies* 101 (2017): 10–22.

195 *Humor, from a neurological perspective*: Janet M. Gibson, "Laughing Is Good for Your Mind and Your Body: Here's What the Research Shows," *The Conversation*, November 23, 2020, https://theconversation.com/laughing-is-good-for-your-mind-and-your-body-heres-what-the-research-shows-145984.

195 *Humor is also thought*: Giovanni Sabato, "What's So Funny? The Science of Why We Laugh," *Scientific American*, June 26, 2019, https://www.scientificamerican.com/article/whats-so-funny-the-science-of-why-we-laugh.

195 *"an unexpected violation"*: Pascal Vrticka, Jessica M. Black, and Allan L. Reiss, "The Neural Basis of Humour Processing," *Nature Reviews Neuroscience* (2013), doi: 10.1038/nrn3566.

196 *"The ability to generate"*: Joseph Polimeni and Jeffrey Reiss, "The First Joke: Exploring the Evolutionary Origins of Humor," *Evolutionary Psychology* 4 (2006), doi: 10.1177/147470490600400129.

197 *happiest countries*: Oshan Jarow, "The World's Emotional Status Is Actually Pretty Good, a New Global Report Finds," *Vox*, July 3, 2024, https://www.vox.com/future-perfect/358022/global-mental-health-happiness-measure-gdp.

198 *"For as long as people have been"*: Sonaiya Kelley, "The Rise and Fall of Cancel Culture in Comedy," *Los Angeles Times*, December 12, 2022, https://www.latimes.com/entertainment-arts/movies/story/2022–12–12/cancel-culture-comedy-emergence.

198 *comedy historian Kliph Nesteroff*: Sonaiya Kelley, "5 Comics Who Were Arrested Onstage," *Los Angeles Times*, December 12, 2022, https://www.latimes.com/entertainment-arts/movies/story/2022–12–12/5-comics-arrested-onstage.

199 *"That* All in the Family *not only"*: Ronald Brownstein, "The Show That Changed Television Forever," *The Atlantic*, March 23, 2021, https://www.theatlantic.com/politics/archive/2021/03/how-all-family-changed-american-tv-forever/618353.

199 *protests at Netflix*: Zoe Christen Jones, "Netflix Employees Stage Walkout over Dave Chappelle Special," *CBS News*, October 25, 2021, https://www.cbsnews.com/news/dave-chappelle-netflix-employees-walkout.

200 *"There are real people"*: Matt Wilstein, "How Comedian Tom Papa Knows Cancel Culture Is 'Very Real,'" *Daily Beast*, December 9, 2022, https://www.thedailybeast.com/how-comedian-tom-papa-knows-cancel-culture-is-very-real.

200 *"While they have a claim"*: Phillip Deen, "What Could It Mean to Say That Today's Stand-Up Audiences Are Too Sensitive?," *The Journal of Aesthetics and Art Criticism* 78 (2020): 501–12, doi: 10.1111/jaac.12755.

201 *political polarization tends to*: Elizabeth N. Simas, Scott Clifford, and Justin H. Kirkland, "How Empathic Concern Fuels Political Polarization," *American Political Science Review* (2020): 258–69.

201 *"humor perception" is lower*: Feng Jiang, Su Lu, Tonglin Jiang, and Heqi Jia, "Does the Relation Between Humor Styles and Subjective Well-Being Vary Across Culture and Age?: A Meta-Analysis," *Frontiers in Psychology* 11 (2020), doi: 10.3389/fpsyg.2020.02213.

Chapter 10: The Capital of Complex Thinkers

208 *In psychology there is a term*: Jenara Nerenberg, *Divergent Mind: Thriving in a World That Wasn't Designed for You* (New York: HarperOne, 2020).

211 *As Dutch researchers*: Alain Van Hiel and Ivan Mervielde, "The Measurement of Cognitive Complexity and Its Relationship with Political Extremism," *Advances in Political Psychology* 24, no. 4 (2003): 781–801.

212 *I highly value honest*: Andrew Jason Cohen, "Psychological Harm and Free Speech on Campus," *Society* 54 (2017): 320–25, doi: 10.1007/s12115-017-0145-6.

219 *"Globalization and the Liminal"*: Lauren Langman and Katie Cangemi, "Globalization and the Liminal: Transgression, Identity and the Urban Primitive," *Research in Urban Policy* 9 (2003): 141–76, doi: 10.1016/S1479-3520(03)09004-4.

223 *"Identity is not a truth"*: Pihla Siim, "Family in Transition: Transnational Family Ties and Identity Negotiation," *Pro Ethnologia* 15 (2004).

224 *"Identity structures also appear"*: Jane Kroger, "What Transits in an Identity Status Transition?," *Identity* 3 (2003): 197–220, doi: 10.1207/S1532706XID0303_02.

224 *"Social identity is expressed"*: Javier A. Salazar, "Analyzing Social Identity (Re) Production: Identity Liminal Events in MMORPGs," *Journal of Virtual Worlds Research* (2008), doi: 10.4101/jvwr.v1i3.353.

225 *"In transnational and multicultural"*: Pihla Siim, "Family in Transition."

225 *"Social movements are liminal phenomena"*: Guobin Yang, "The Liminal Effects of Social Movements: Red Guards and the Transformation of Identity," *Sociological Forum* 15, no. 3 (2000): 379–406, doi: 10.1023/A:1007563225473.

227 *"You end up isolated"*: Sherry Turkle, *Alone Together: Why We Expect More from Technology and Less from Each Other* (New York: Basic Books, 2011).